The Standards-Based Classroom

The Standards-Based Classroom

Make Learning the Goal

Emily Rinkema and Stan Williams
Foreword by Ken O'Connor

CORWIN
A SAGE Publishing Company

FOR INFORMATION:

Corwin
A SAGE Company
2455 Teller Road
Thousand Oaks, California 91320
(800) 233-9936
www.corwin.com

SAGE Publications Ltd.
1 Oliver's Yard
55 City Road
London EC1Y 1SP
United Kingdom

SAGE Publications India Pvt. Ltd.
B 1/I 1 Mohan Cooperative Industrial Area
Mathura Road, New Delhi 110 044
India

SAGE Publications Asia-Pacific Pte. Ltd.
3 Church Street
#10-04 Samsung Hub
Singapore 049483

Program Director: Jessica Allan
Associate Editor: Lucas Schleicher
Editorial Assistant: Mia Rodriguez
Production Editor: Tori Mirsadjadi
Copy Editor: Erin Livingston
Typesetter: C&M Digitals (P) Ltd.
Proofreader: Dennis Webb
Indexer: Maria Sosnowski
Cover Designer: Candice Harman
Marketing Manager: Margaret O'Connor

Library of Congress Cataloging-in-Publication Data

Names: Rinkema, Emily, author. | Williams, Stan, 1970- author.

Title: The Standards-Based Classroom : Make Learning the Goal / Emily Rinkema and Stan Williams ; Foreword by Ken O'Connor.

Description: Thousand Oaks, California : Corwin, a SAGE Company, [2019] | Includes bibliographical references and index.

Identifiers: LCCN 2018015851 | ISBN 9781544324203 (pbk. : alk. paper)

Subjects: LCSH: Education—Standards—United States. | Education—Curricula—Standards—United States. | Educational tests and measurements—United States.

Classification: LCC LB3060.83 .R56 2018 | DDC 379.1/58—dc23

LC record available at https://lccn.loc.gov/2018015851

This book is printed on acid-free paper.

23 24 25 26   10 9 8 7 6

Contents

Foreword

I had the pleasure of meeting Emily Rinkema for the first time at the Corwin Assessment Institute in Chicago in October 2017. I met Stan for the first time at the ASCD Annual Conference in Boston in March 2018. At the ASCD conference, I was fortunate to copresent with Emily and Stan (along with Doug Reeves, Lee Ann Jung, and Brian Stack) and saw firsthand their commitment to standards-based learning (SBL) and their expert knowledge and willingness to help others. Prior to meeting them, I had followed Emily and Stan for several years through their very helpful Champlain Valley Union (CVU) Learns website (cvulearns.weebly.com), their CVU Learns blog (cvulearnsblog.blogspot.com), and their contributions to the Standards-Based Learning and Grading Facebook group and the Standards-Based Learning Twitter chat (#sblchat), so I was thrilled when they said they were writing a book and asked for a recommendation for a publisher. I recommended Corwin, and I was excited when they told me that their book proposal was accepted. I was honored and immensely pleased when they asked me to write their foreword. I was totally blown away when I read their manuscript because the book is so clever and funny (in a droll way) and, above all, so practical and packed with great advice on how to implement SBL.

Over the last twenty-four years, as I have worked with and watched schools and districts move toward SBL, grading, and reporting (SBLG&R), two mistakes have been most prevalent. The first mistake is beginning with revising grading procedures and/or the report card before the *why* has been clearly established with teachers, students, parents, and the community. The second common mistake is lack of clarity, understanding, and consistency with performance standards, especially with levels rather than the familiar points and percentages.

This book superbly addresses the first problem through the order of the four sections, starting with Section 1: Articulate Desired Results, Section 2: Develop Targeted Assessments, Section 3: Design Effective Instruction, and Section 4: Monitor and Communicate Learning. This gets the order of operations right by establishing the need for assessment and instruction to be based on clearly described and understood standards (both the *what* and the *how well*), so the *why* for communicating learning through standards-based grading and reporting is simply a logical conclusion of what is happening in standards-based instruction and assessment.

The second problem is addressed through the superb performance standards that Emily and Stan have developed. They call these *learning scales*, which are scales that describe progressions from novice to advanced; they "guide instruction and provide feedback along the way, as well as assess achievement at the end." There are several unique and brilliant features of the scales: First, they have no labels or numbers, so they force everyone involved to focus on the learning; second, they are all positive *I can*–type statements that avoid the negative language that is commonly used to describe the lower levels in rubrics; third, they are very flexible because they are not tied to a particular assessment but allow for use across different grade levels, subjects, and assessments; and fourth, they explain clearly why *with support* or *independently* should not be used to identify differences between the levels in the learning scales. Many examples of scales for different subjects and grade levels are included, but what makes them even more powerful and relevant is that the authors have developed and provided scales for learning progressions in each chapter for teachers as they move toward more effective instruction, assessment, and grading.

Emily and Stan are practitioners who have worked for over eight years to develop effective SBLG&R and, although they have transitioned from the classroom to their current roles as instructional coaches, they still teach a high school class. It is an innovative course called Think Tank (cvuthinktank.weebly.com) that "allows students and teachers to work together to answer questions facing our systems and structures as we continue our transition to a personalized, proficiency-based school." The fact that they have been and still are classroom teachers is reflected in the practical structure of each chapter: a learning scale for the specific context is followed by commentary and context; the practical part (with examples) provides what educators really need to understand. Each chapter ends with identification of challenges and the very helpful and insightful "Guilt-Free Box," where they suggest modifications that teachers can use to make the transition to SBLG&R easier.

Another strength of the book is the emphasis on the need for intentionality in curriculum and instructional design. The framework for this is provided by K-U-D charts for each unit or course (and the book!) that identify what students (and readers) will *know, understand* and be able to *do* at the end of a unit/course (or the book). As with everything in the book, the K-U-D charts are extremely practical: they aren't laundry lists of every little thing but instead focus on the essential learnings.

Given their experience and expertise, I'm also impressed with how humble Stan and Emily are in their generous acknowledgment of the authors and speakers from whom they have learned in the "Further Exploration" part in each section. They also acknowledge that their use of terminology may be different from others by providing a glossary of key terms in each section, and I particularly appreciate that they identify the difference between grades and scores in the same way that I do!

These authors are very understanding of the differences among teachers, schools, and districts, so the book is an easy must-read for all educators, including those who are considering moving to SBLG&R and, most importantly, for those who have tried to implement SBLG&R and have given up to varying extents, because it provides a road map for effective implementation and for the correction or avoidance of implementation errors. It is also a must-read for educators who are implementing SBLG&R because it provides affirmation for many of the practices while providing ways that these educators can tweak their practices to make them even better. While it is not specifically a book for leaders, I also think it is a must-read for district and school administrators because it provides what leaders need to know so they can support teachers who are implementing SBLG&R. For the same reasons, it is a book that should be read by school board members, policy makers, and parents who need to understand and value SBLG&R.

All I can say in conclusion is thank you to Emily and Stan for a great book that provides brilliant practical information and advice. Schools will be better places for learning because of your work and your willingness to share.

Ken O'Connor,
The Villages, Florida and Scarborough, Ontario, Canada
April 2018

Acknowledgments

First, we would not have written this book or survived the past five years if it weren't for our coaching and teaching colleagues, Monica Carter and Jessica Lemieux, two of the finest educators we have ever met. We are a team, celebrating together when things are great, supporting each other when things aren't, collaborating to solve problems, and constantly challenging each other to think creatively. Monica's logical approach, calm presence, and fierce loyalty, and Jess's curiosity, honesty, and determination inspire and ground us daily. We thank them for making Office 131 a place where an elephant, a honey badger, a border collie, and an ostrich can continue to laugh, cry, and learn together.

Second, none of this work would be possible or worthy of sharing if it were not for the leaders in our district who used their vision, bravery, and hard work to establish foundations, to build community buy-in, to support passionate and innovative educators, and to remove obstacles to implementation. Thanks to Val Gardner, Sean McMannon, Jeff Evans, and Adam Bunting for incredible leadership as principals; to Katherine Riley and Jeff Evans for their leadership as directors of instruction and curriculum; and to Elaine Pinckney for her leadership as superintendent. Change is not easy, and all of these leaders brought (and continue to bring) their skills, wisdom, and humor to the work in our district and across our state.

Third, the teachers at Champlain Valley Union (CVU) and in the Champlain Valley School District (CVSD) are incredible. Their professionalism, willingness to take risks, and flexibility are not only what make this a great place to work but are also what make the district a great place to be a learner. There are too many to call out by name, but we want to send out a particular thanks to the original CWG (you know who you are) for taking that initial risk eight years ago that led to all this change.

Fourth, we want to thank the students in our inaugural Think Tank class—Abigail, Annabelle, Beckett, Bobby, Charlie, Cianna, Ella, Emma, Julia, Kate, Lindsey, Luca, Maddie, Mia, the Nathans, Olivia, Sabine, and Sadie—who remind us daily why we love teaching and what school has the potential to become. We know they will keep learning, keep challenging assumptions, and continue to embrace those cognitive conflicts. Oh . . . and they are going to change the world.

Finally, there is no way we would have survived the last eight years or written this book if it weren't for the people we live with. Emily thanks her amazing husband, Bill, for his dedication to education, his belief in public school teachers, and his willingness to grapple with the toughest questions facing our profession. Perhaps more importantly, she thanks him for patiently listening, for making her laugh, for making the best gin and tonic in the world, and for always being her favorite human being. Stan thanks his best friend and wife, Naomi, because—let's be honest—if it wasn't for her, he would be sitting in a small apartment on East Avenue playing fantasy sports, watching *Shameless*, surrounded by turkey bacon sub wrappers and empty bottles. He also thanks his wonderful son, Sam, and his amazing daughter, Lily, who have taught him what it means to love life, soccer, and reality TV and who remind him daily why this work is so important.

PUBLISHER'S ACKNOWLEDGMENTS

Corwin gratefully acknowledges the contributions of the following reviewers:

Dr. Becca Lindahl, Professional Learning and Leadership Consultant
Heartland AEA 11
Johnston, IA

Brian M. Stack, High School Principal
Sanborn Regional High School
Kingston, NH

Garnet Hillman, Author and Educational Consultant
Hillman Consulting
Crest Hill, IL

Dr. Tom Buckmiller, Professor of Education
Drake University
Des Moines, IA

Dr. Ken Darvall, Principal
Tima International School
Craignish, QLD, Australia

Hope Edlin, Grade 5 Teacher
Bethel Elementary
Simpsonville, SC

Matthew Drewette-Card, Director of Curriculum, Instruction, Assessment
Maine Alternative Organizational Structure No. 94
Dexter, ME

Dr. Carol A. Commodore, Educational Consultant
Leadership, Learning and Assessment, LLC
Oconomowoc, WI

Renee Peoples, Teaching and Learning Coach
Swain County Schools
Bryson City, NC

Brad Latzke, Education Consultant
Shanghai American School—Puxi Campus
Minhang Qu, Shanghai Shi, China

Hugh O'Donnell, Education Consultant
Mentor Learning, LLC
Bend, OR

Katie Budrow, Science Teacher
Caruso Middle School
Deerfield, IL

Jay McTighe, Author and Consultant
McTighe and Associates
Columbia, MD

Matt Townsley, Director of Instruction
Solon Community Schools
Solon, IA

Derek Oldfield, Assistant Principal
Hedgesville High School
Hedgesville, WV

About the Authors

Emily Rinkema is currently an instructional coach in the Champlain Valley School District (CVSD) in Vermont, spending half of her time supporting standards-based instruction and learning at the high school and the other half supporting the middle schools in their transition to standards-based learning (SBL). She also code-signed and coteaches Think Tank, a class that puts high school students at the center of the educational transformation happening around them. Emily began teaching English and humanities at Champlain Valley Union High School twenty years ago and was inspired by the progressive philosophy of the school and community from the start. While teaming with Stan Williams in a heterogeneous tenth-grade humanities class, they became obsessed with differentiated instruction and SBL, applied for a sabbatical, and began down the path that would lead to instructional coaching. Emily is the cofounder of the Vermont Standards-Based Learning (VTSBL) Collective, a grassroots organization that brings together educators interested in improving education through SBL. She has organized, led, and participated in the annual symposium sponsored by the VTSBL Collective and has presented about SBL at schools around Vermont and at the 2018 ASCD Empower18 Conference. Emily has a master's degree in English from the Bread Loaf School of English at Middlebury College and is still involved with the Bread Loaf Teacher Network and, along with Stan, is very active professionally on social media through @ CVULearns.

Stan Williams has taught and worked in the Champlain Valley School District (CVSD) for over twenty years. Currently, he is working as an instructional coach for the district and spends his time supporting standards-based learning (SBL) and instruction at the high school and the four district middle schools. Besides his work as an instructional coach, Stan coteaches a class called Think Tank, which has students examining education and learning and has kids at the heart of educational transformation. Over his time teaching, Stan has worked side by side with Emily Rinkema. Together, they have team-taught multiple classes and have shared a great interest in differentiated instruction. It was working with Emily on differentiation during a yearlong sabbatical that educated him on the importance of and need for standards-based education. Stan has presented to teachers, college students, and administrators around the state and has been a regular contributor at the annual Vermont Standards-Based Learning (VTSBL) Symposium. He also presented at the 2018 ASCD Empower18 Conference. In 2017, Stan won Nellie Mae's Lawrence O'Toole Teacher Leadership Award for his work creating student-led middle school think tanks and the Think Tank class at the high school. Stan received his undergraduate degree from Hamilton College and did his graduate work at Saint Michael's College. He is active professionally, along with Emily, on social media through @CVULearns.

Introduction

Before we get to what this book is about, we want to be clear what this book is not about.

First, this is not a book about standards-based grading. There are so many fantastic books out there already that clearly explain the *why* and *how* of changing grading practices. If you are looking for specifics about changing from traditional, 19th century grading practices to brain-based, 21st century grading practices, start with authors Ken O'Connor, Thomas Guskey, and Rick Wormeli and then join the Standards-Based Learning and Grading Facebook page and the Wednesday night #sblchat on Twitter. Though we have a chapter on grading and reporting, we are going to assume that our readers already have an understanding of the *why* and *how* of these important changes, despite the institutional difficulties in making them happen.

Second, this is not a book about the need for significant educational change. If you are looking for transformational inspiration or facts to support the immediacy of the need for this cultural change, then start with thinkers such as Sir Ken Robinson, Tony Wagner, Ted Dintersmith, George Couros, or Alfie Kohn. We are going to assume our readers understand why schools can't stay the same and why teaching can no longer look like it did one hundred years ago, when we were children, when we first started teaching, or even last year. We are already on the verge of being too late for this generation of learners.

Finally, this is not a book about getting it right. We'll be honest with you up front: Shifting to standards-based instruction and learning is not going to go smoothly. It's going to be messy and rocky and contentious and uncomfortable. You will get things wrong. You will make mistakes. You will say things you don't mean to say to colleagues and students and parents. You will get questions you can't answer, face challenges you can't immediately respond to, and have uncomfortable conflicts (with others and with yourself). You may even grapple with why you became a teacher and whether this is all worth it. So, we are going to assume that you are comfortable taking risks, making mistakes, and struggling through the mud of learning. In other words, we're going to assume you are comfortable modeling to your students what it means to be a learner.

If you haven't yet set the book down, then here's what you have in your hand. This is a book about standards-based teaching and learning, the practices related to curriculum, instruction, and assessment that are essential to improving learning in a standards-based classroom. It's a book about practical implementation, the how-to of the classroom. It's a book that provides one way to begin making changes that will allow the types of transformation those other books so beautifully describe.

Our intent is to provide *a* way—not *the* way—to implement standards-based learning (SBL) in the classroom. As we have immersed ourselves in the world of SBL for the past eight years—first as high school teachers, and now as both teachers and instructional coaches at the middle and high school level—we have experimented with and revised and picked and chosen and synthesized and created and adapted many strategies and suggestions into a version of SBL that is effective in our context and for our community of learners. The ideas in this book are not new and mostly are not our own; we are practicing on the shoulders of giants, using the hard work and ideas of thinkers such as Carol Tomlinson, Rick Wormeli, Thomas Guskey, Ken O'Connor, Rick Stiggins, James Zull, Lee Ann Jung, Bill Rich, Grant Wiggins, and Richard DuFour (among so many others!) to build systems and structures and strategies and tools to make it all work. Three years from now, our version of SBL will look very different. Our teachers will continue experimenting, revising, picking, choosing, synthesizing, creating, and adapting based on new understandings of the brain, different needs in the community, or increased knowledge gained from experts and practitioners. As this happens, our version of SBL will continue to change and grow and improve, as it must if we want to continue to improve learning for our students.

That said, this is the best we know now, and so we will share our way in hopes that teachers in other communities can use it to find theirs. Every community is different, and each school has its own history, structures, and mandates; these differences may require shifts in both the *what* and the *how* of implementation. We encourage you to take what can work, adapt what's close, revise what's not relevant, and table what's not currently possible. We don't expect that our ideas will work for everyone, just as the ideas of others did not always work for us, but we hope they offer a place to start building your own ideas.

We can't stress enough that the changes involved in transitioning to SBL are difficult, and they can challenge fundamental beliefs about teaching and learning that we have held throughout our lives. In a standards-based class, what we teach is irrelevant if we can't ensure that our students learn, so our primary role becomes facilitator, monitor, and designer of learning, rather than deliverer of content. For those of us who got into teaching because we love our discipline areas, we may need to let go of our control around content, and this can be particularly difficult. In a standards-based class, learning becomes the constant and time the variable.

For those of us still working in traditional systems, we may need to find ways to bend rules or manipulate programs in the name of learning, and this can be difficult. In a standards-based class, grades are no longer used as currency, so we will need to understand adolescent motivation, build new habits of learning (theirs and ours), and develop strategies to help everyone see learning as the goal. For those of us who have relied on grades as rewards and punishments—which includes our students—this can be particularly difficult.

If it's going to be that messy and that difficult, then why do it?

Well, as we said earlier, we are going to assume that you believe in the big-picture *whys* already; that you understand the societal need for innovation in our profession, just as every other profession; that you believe our students not only *deserve* better but *need* better in order to be prepared for their futures; and that you are frustrated with the limitations of the current systems and structures. So, we are going to give you one more *why*, and it's not big or societal or philosophical: It's Jessica S. Or it's Erika B. Or it's Carter L. or Dylan R. or Nathan V.B. or Eva R. or Feston A. or Taya L. or Nawal A. It's every student in your class who deserves the best you have to give.

The absolute best way to improve student learning is to deeply know and care about each and every one of our learners. It's to believe in them, to challenge them, and to expose them to ideas they didn't know they cared about. It's to listen to them, to hold them accountable to their best selves, and to give them many chances to practice skills they will need throughout their lives. It's to show them we care. We don't need SBL to do any of that, and if we had to choose for our own children between a teacher who cared deeply about our kids or one who had perfect pedagogy, we would choose the first every time. But we believe we can have both—we believe that SBL helps us get to know our learners at a depth that traditional teaching rarely allowed. We believe that SBL helps us provide the practice our learners need to be and to become their best selves. And we believe that SBL holds us accountable to our students and their success more than ever before.

HOW TO USE THIS BOOK

We have organized the book into four sections: Articulate Desired Results, Develop Targeted Assessment, Design Effective Instruction, and Monitor and Communicate Learning. While each can be read and used on its own, the parts and their individual chapters all work together to form a complete system of implementation. There is an interdependence among parts that cannot easily come across in the linear format of a book, so please understand that the art of teaching and learning mixes these steps as necessary (see Figure 0.1 on the next page).

FIGURE 0.1   How the Four Sections of This Book Are Interrelated

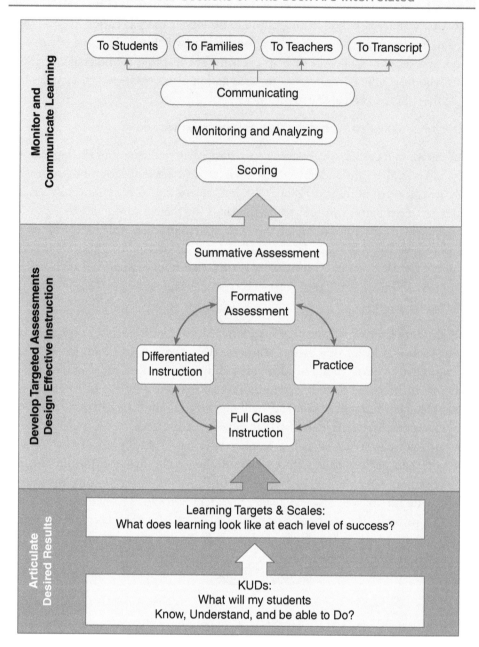

Each section begins with a brief overview, a glossary of significant terms, and further resources for exploration:

- **Glossary of Key Terms**: We decided to define the major terms we are using in each chapter. All of these terms exist outside of this book, and we think it's important to understand how we are using them in our context. All are further defined within the chapters, as are many other relevant terms.

- **Further Exploration:** As we wrote in our introduction, our work with SBL would not be possible or effective without the work of so many others. Each chapter is based on the ideas of other thinkers, experts, and educational innovators, and so we have chosen to highlight two who have been most influential to our process. These lists are by no means exhaustive, and we encourage you to ask the people you admire who has influenced them. Our biggest hope with this part of each chapter is that it will inspire you to read more. Our work skims the surface of each of these elements, and when you are ready to get below that surface—or if our ideas don't quite make sense—then we want you to dive deeper.

Within the sections, each chapter has the following parts:

- **A Learning Scale:** What we know about good learning applies to all learners, not only our students. Teachers learning new pedagogical strategies need clear targets and articulated scales as much as students need to learn new skills in science class. To help provide this clarity, we worked with teachers throughout our district to create scales for teachers transitioning from traditional learning environments to SBL environments. We have used the scales to organize our chapters, breaking a complex system into smaller, slightly less complex parts.

- **Commentary and Context:** We do not pretend to be impartial about the ideas in this book. We have very strong beliefs, based on our experiences and the experiences of teachers we have worked with over the past eight years. We will share these beliefs at the beginning of each chapter. In addition to commentary, we use the first part of each chapter to provide any necessary context for the specific element of SBL and the definitions of the terms and concepts as we use them. You will notice that our definitions may vary at times from other thinkers and practitioners, so we try to be clear in order to avoid confusion.

- **The Practical Part (With Examples):** Let's face it, we know most of you bought this book because of this part. "Enough already with everything else, just tell me how to do it!" In each chapter, we will tell you how we did it and provide steps to begin implementation. We made a lot of mistakes to get to the point where we had practical advice to give, and all of the how-tos in the book are based on years of getting it wrong, then partially right, then to the point of effectiveness. While our background and personal experience is in high school humanities, we have tried to include examples that span from fifth to twelfth grade and across as many disciplines as possible. You will not find an example in your discipline in all chapters, so be creative in your thinking of how to transfer the central ideas to your own teaching situation.

- **Challenges:** We could write an entire book on the challenges, but in order to maintain some optimism, we limited ourselves to two specific challenges per chapter. You will notice that some of the challenges repeat (though play out in slightly different ways) and others are very specific to a strategy. These challenges were the ones our community faced, and understanding them may help you avoid obstacles or, at least, be prepared when they pop up.

- **The Guilt-Free Box:** This is a suggestion for starting if you are feeling overwhelmed, under-supported, or thoroughly exhausted. It's a recognition that this work is difficult, and that sometimes compromise is necessary in order to maintain the capacity for compassion, humor, and change. The goal is progress, not perfection.

In addition, we have included a K-U-D for the entire book and all of the scales together in one place. We have used these scales with faculties and individual teachers to pre-assess and determine prior knowledge. We have found them to be an effective way to differentiate professional development based on need or on interest, and they can also be used for ongoing self-assessment or to guide individual goals. The scales can also hold administration and teacher leaders accountable as we plan our department meetings, faculty meetings, or other professional learning opportunities. Just as we ask our teachers to be clear about their purpose and targets with students, those leading need to be clear with teachers about the same.

You can read the book from beginning to end or you can jump around based on need or interest, but please understand that the parts cannot exist without each other. SBL is a system of learning, and we will reference earlier elements throughout the book that are at the core of implementation.

Finally, you are welcome to use or adapt anything in this book. Teaching is hard enough, so if there is anything in here that will help make life easier, have at it.

Thanks for reading, and best of luck. Our students are worth it.

Standards-Based Learning in the Classroom: The K-U-D

AFTER FINISHING THIS BOOK, WE HOPE OUR READERS KNOW . . .	AFTER FINISHING THIS BOOK, WE HOPE OUR READERS UNDERSTAND THAT . . .	AFTER FINISHING THIS BOOK, WE HOPE OUR READERS ARE ABLE TO BEGIN TO . . .
strategies and tools for effective teaching and learning in a standards-based classroom, including • K-U-Ds, • learning targets, • scales, • practice and formative assessments, • summative assessments, • strategies for instructional design, • differentiated instruction, • gradebook structures, • tools for tracking learning, and • systems for communicating learning.	students can meet any target that they can see and that stands still for them (Stiggins, 2017). knowing where students are in relation to our targets ensures that we can provide the instruction, practice, and feedback necessary for learning. we are responsible for providing appropriate instruction to *all* of our students, not only the easy ones. scores and grades are communication tools, not compensation tools. progress, not perfection, is the goal.	use unit K-U-Ds to drive instruction and assessment. create/use learning targets that are scalable and transferable within and/or across units. develop/use instructional scales for each learning target that define the increasing complexity of the skill progression. work with special educators to understand how students' learning profiles may impact their achievement, and accommodate, modify, and plan to support their success on learning targets. design summative assessments that provide reliable, individual evidence of student achievement of the K-U-D. design non-scored practice activities and intentional formative assessments to provide reliable, individual evidence of achievement toward learning targets. introduce and model skills that will be assessed, and design tasks that allow students to use these skills to practice the content. differentiate instruction and/or activities based on data from formative assessments in order to move all students forward on the scales. maintain a gradebook that tracks summative achievement of learning targets on a 1–4 scale; score assessments using the same scale. communicate clearly and efficiently with all students and families about progress and learning.

ARTICULATE DESIRED RESULTS

I have course curriculum documents.	I have course K-U-Ds and unit descriptions and/or expectations.	**I use unit K-U-Ds to drive my instruction and assessment.**	I use my unit K-U-Ds with students to clearly communicate goals and expectations for learning.
I create/use learning targets that assess specific content and/ or are mostly discrete tasks or activities.	I create/use learning targets that are scalable (complexity can be raised or lowered).	**I create/use learning targets that are scalable and transferable within and/or across units.**	I create/use learning targets that are aligned and calibrated within common courses or across disciplines.
I provide descriptions of my expectations for assignments.	I develop/use rubrics that list or describe expectations for assignments.	**I develop/use instructional scales for each of my learning targets that define the increasing complexity of the skill progression.**	I develop/use benchmark sheets with exemplars to show each level of progression.
I allow/expect special educators to modify or accommodate my curriculum for students.	I work with special educators to encourage work completion and access to accommodations in my class.	**I work with special educators to understand how students' learning profiles may impact their achievement in my class and accommodate, modify, and plan to support their success on my learning targets.**	I collaborate with special educators in order to intentionally maximize the student's strengths and improve upon both the student's individual goals and my class's learning targets.

DEVELOP TARGETED ASSESSMENT

I design summative assessments that mostly address knowledge of my unit or course content.	I design summative assessments that provide evidence of student achievement of the K-U-D.	**I design summative assessments that provide reliable, individual evidence of student achievement of the K-U-D.**	I design summative assessments that allow students to demonstrate achievement of the K-U-D in an authentic, engaging way.
I design formative assessments related to my content.	I provide practice time and design formative assessments that are related to my content and learning targets.	**I design non-scored practice activities and intentional formative assessments to provide reliable, individual evidence of achievement toward learning targets.**	I design a variety of individual and collaborative practice activities that encourage risk taking; my formative assessments provide reliable, individual evidence of achievement toward learning targets in a way that matches or builds how students will be have summative assessments.

DESIGN EFFECTIVE INSTRUCTION

Most of my instructional time focuses on content delivery.	I split my instructional time between content delivery and student activities.	**I introduce and model skills that will be assessed and design tasks that allow students to use these skills to practice the content.**	I directly instruct the skills my students will need to acquire and apply deep content knowledge.
I encourage students who are struggling with my learning targets to get help outside of class.	I use class time to differentiate instruction and/or activities for students who struggle with my learning targets.	**I differentiate instruction and/or activities based on data from formative assessments in order to move all students forward on my scales.**	I use a variety of strategies, structures, and models to differentiate instruction and/or activities for all students.

MONITOR AND COMMUNICATE LEARNING

I maintain a gradebook organized around assignments or assessment categories; I grade assessments using percentages or points.	I maintain a gradebook organized around learning targets; I grade assessments using percentages or points and convert them to a 1-4 scale for my gradebook.	**I maintain a gradebook that tracks the summative achievement of learning targets on a 1-4 scale; I score assessments using the same scale.**	I maintain a gradebook that tracks formative and summative achievement of learning targets on a 1-4 scale; I use my gradebook to analyze achievement data and drive instructional choices.
I communicate with families on set grading/reporting dates when they contact me with concerns or questions.	I communicate with families on set grading/reporting dates and when/if I see there is an issue in my class.	**I communicate clearly and efficiently with all students and families about progress and learning.**	I have a comprehensive communication plan that includes learning, personal, curriculum, and habits.

SECTION I

Articulate Desired Results

The brain wants to know where it's going. In order to learn most effectively, we need to know our destination. Grant Wiggins and Jay McTighe studied the principles of curriculum design years ago, and their findings still remain true: Students (and adults) want a clear purpose for learning; they want to know where they are going and why they are going there. They developed their findings into one of the most transformational systems in recent education: *understanding by design*, also known as *backward design*. Whether you read Marzano, Wormeli, O'Connor, Wiggins, Fisher, Guskey, the Heath brothers, Jensen, or Zull, they all agree with Wiggins and McTighe on the importance of clarity of purpose. In other words, this isn't new, and it isn't experimental. Having a clear, articulated goal improves learning; knowing where we want to be at the end helps us get there.

[GLOSSARY OF KEY TERMS]

K-U-D: A K-U-D is a curriculum-planning document based on the idea that knowing where we want to end up will help us get there more effectively. This specific format was developed by Carol Ann Tomlinson and articulates what students will *know* (K), *understand* (U), and be able to *do* (D) at the end of a period of learning.

Learning Target: As we define them, *learning targets* are the skills (Ds from the K-U-D) that we want students to have at the end of a period of learning. These are skills that students will use to demonstrate their knowledge and understanding of our content, and they are the skills that we will intentionally instruct, practice, assess, and report on throughout our units or courses.

Learning Scale: Our learning targets live in a continuum of skill progression called a *scale*. The scale shows how the targeted skill becomes more complex as it moves from left to right on the scale and allows us to shift our instruction as appropriate for our learners. The learning scale is used for instruction, feedback, and assessment.

(Continued)

(Continued)

Accommodation Versus Modification: When collaborating with special educators, we may need to accommodate or modify our targets and scales based on learner profiles and individualized plans. When we accommodate, we do not change the language or intent of the target; we apply proven accommodations that allow our students to reach or surpass our targets. We modify targets when the language and intent of the target is inappropriate for our learners; when accommodations are not enough to allow access to success on our targets, modifications become appropriate.

FURTHER EXPLORATION

Carol Tomlinson: While Tomlinson has dozens of excellent books that include chapters about K-U-Ds, they are no substitute for seeing and hearing her in person, if possible. Her wisdom, calm presence, and depth of understanding about learning inspired many of the teachers at our school who went on to pilot standards-based learning (SBL) in their courses. If you cannot bring her to your area or travel to one of her conferences, start with *The Differentiated Classroom* (2016), *Differentiation in Practice*, or *Integrating Differentiated Instruction & Understanding by Design* (coauthored by Jay McTighe) (2006).

Grant Wiggins and Jay McTighe: The idea of backward design is central to the creation of K-U-Ds, so any of the resources by Wiggins or Jay McTighe will help with the fundamental understanding of the *why* and *how* of approaching learning this way. Start with *Integrating Differentiated Instruction & Understanding by Design* (2006), a book that should be in every educator's bookcase anyway.

Connie Moss and Susan Brookhart: In their book, *Learning Targets: Helping Students Aim for Understanding in Today's Lesson* (2012), Moss and Brookhart explore the importance of concrete targets to the learning process. Though their definition of *learning targets* differs a bit from our approach (they write about daily targets), the underlying purpose and beliefs are the same. Their work on formative assessment is also excellent.

Rick Stiggins: Rick Stiggins will pop up in the next section as well, as his influence on our work has been significant. While we rely heavily on his ideas about assessment, we include him here so that you might read his chapter on learning targets and his strategies for deconstructing standards in *Classroom Assessment for Student Learning*, coauthored by Jan Chappuis, Steve Chappuis, and Judith Arter (2012). More about him in the next section!

Bill Rich: Bill Rich is a Vermont education consultant specializing in brain-based learning and teaching. His work with learning scales has been instrumental in our state, and he runs full-day workshops to support teachers in the development of effective instructional scales that support our state's move to proficiency-based learning. He has great resources and links at his website (www.redhouselearning.com).

Lee Ann Jung: Whether writing and speaking about learning in general, proficiency-based grading, or students with special needs, Lee Ann Jung is direct, concise, eloquent, and inspirational. As with many of the other authors we have noted, if you get a chance to see her in person, take it. Regardless, you should get this book immediately: *Grading Exceptional and Struggling Learners* (cowritten with Thomas Guskey) (2012). This book will answer your questions about grading and scoring, about legal implications and requirements, and about what it means to be fair in your assessment and grading practices.

CHAPTER 1

Developing K-U-Ds

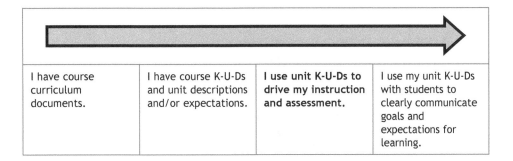

I have course curriculum documents.	I have course K-U-Ds and unit descriptions and/or expectations.	**I use unit K-U-Ds to drive my instruction and assessment.**	I use my unit K-U-Ds with students to clearly communicate goals and expectations for learning.

COMMENTARY AND CONTEXT

Backward design is the foundation of Carol Tomlinson's work with differentiated instruction, and it is through her work that we were first introduced to the K-U-D structure that has become the backbone of standards-based learning (SBL) at our school. This curriculum document articulates what we want students to *know*, *understand*, and be able to *do* at the end of a period of learning. It allows us to set a clear destination so that we can more intentionally and flexibly plan paths to help students get there.

When we think back to our early days of teaching together, it's hard to remember how we decided what to teach. We knew we were going to teach about Gilgamesh or Sumerian civilizations, but beyond that, we were sort of flying without a radar. Sometimes we had materials from previous years, sometimes we had an idea for a cool project, and sometimes we relied on reading the textbook the night before class and hoping for inspiration. Conversely, a friend who began her teaching career in another state told us how she was handed a three-inch binder of lesson plans that she was expected to teach. She was given a detailed pacing guide, told what page of the textbook to be on what date, and provided state-designed assessments she was required to give. These are both extreme examples of curricular design. Our experience allowed for great personalization and autonomy but provided no accountability or direction; our friend's experience provided both accountability and direction but did not allow for variation based on interest or learning (the student's or the teacher's).

When the K-U-D came into our lives over a decade ago, we were ready for it. Having autonomy was great, but we both recognized the need for a bit more intentionality in our curricular and instructional design. By no means did we want or need the three-inch binder, but we craved something that would drive our choices and force us to be intentional about our teaching. We needed a clearer destination.

When we first started using K-U-Ds, they were pretty rough. We tried to pack everything we did into the new format and came out with pages and pages of bulleted pieces of knowledge, vague yet lofty understandings, and a list of everything we planned to have students do. Basically, we reorganized existing activities, lesson plans, and assessments into what we hoped would help us improve learning.

It turns out that it's a bit more complicated than that. Over time, we read more, experimented in our classes, went to more conferences, and began to realize that developing an effective, useful K-U-D meant digging into our experiences, plans, and content to determine what really mattered. It became absurd to think that we could actually teach everything (and more absurd to think we could ensure that our students learned it all), so what were our essentials? What were the most leveraging concepts, the ones that students might need in other classes or in their futures? What skills should we focus on now to ensure better learning later? At the end of their time with us, what should our students know, understand, and be able to do? We learned that this document was not meant to be a comprehensive list of every possible direction in a course or unit; rather, it was the North Star that would keep us focused on what was most important.

So, our first and most important advice when implementing SBL in your classroom? Start with a K-U-D.

THE PRACTICAL PART

At its simplest, a K-U-D is what we want learners to *know, understand,* and be able to *do* at the end of the period of learning. We can have unit K-U-Ds, course K-U-Ds, and even department or program K-U-Ds. For the sake of simplicity here, we are going to focus on unit K-U-Ds, but the same principles can be applied to larger or smaller periods of learning.

KNOWS

It's important to understand the difference between content and knowledge. *Content* is what's available, the pool of rich, engaging, relevant information, texts, examples, and events we have to choose from when determining how to best help students demonstrate understanding and skill; *knowledge* is what students know at the end of the period of learning, the content that they have made their own and will be able to use. Knowledge takes time to build. It takes activating prior knowledge, determining relationships and relevance, practicing with ideas individually and collaboratively, and deep understanding. Many math teachers learn about the difference between *procedural knowledge* and *conceptual knowledge*, the first allowing for rote memorization of strategies or simple skills and the latter focusing on deeper relationships among facts. James Hiebert described conceptual knowledge in his 1986 book, *Conceptual and Procedural Knowledge: The Case of Mathematics*, as

> knowledge that is rich in relationships. It can be thought of as a connected web of knowledge, a network in which the linking relationships are as prominent as the discrete pieces of information. Relationships pervade the individual facts and propositions so that all pieces of information are linked to some network. (pp. 3–4)

What's nice about this definition of knowledge is that it supports what we know about deep learning. In a world where we can ask Siri or Alexa to look up discrete facts for us and we can rely on our phones to complete most simple, procedural tasks, it makes sense to be spending our effort in school on developing and expanding conceptual knowledge.

Because most teachers have amazing conceptual knowledge about their content areas, we often start with way too many *knows*. We love all the facts and see them as important. I mean, you can't really understand the importance of the Reformation if you don't know who Huldrych Zwingli is or that it wasn't over until the Peace of Westphalia in 1648! But remember that the *K*s are the essential knowledge that you want all students to use when they are demonstrating their skills and understanding and that you can virtually guarantee they will carry with them beyond the end of the unit. Students will almost certainly be exposed to—and learn—much more content than you list in this column (including Zwingli and Westphalia, perhaps), and your ability to differentiate will increase if you (and they) have access to a rich, varied, and deep pool of content beyond what you list on your K-U-D. But limit your *knows* to what's essential and let go of the urge to list everything that you might possibly cover.

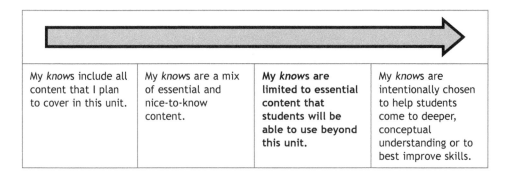

My *knows* include all content that I plan to cover in this unit.	My *knows* are a mix of essential and nice-to-know content.	**My *knows* are limited to essential content that students will be able to use beyond this unit.**	My *knows* are intentionally chosen to help students come to deeper, conceptual understanding or to best improve skills.

UNDERSTANDINGS

Knowing a lot is not enough. It's important for sure, and the more knowledge our students have, the more prepared they will be for learning to come. But if we can ensure deeper understandings that transcend specific content, then our students will be able to use their knowledge to solve problems that don't even exist yet. Lynn Erickson's work around conceptual understanding is an excellent place to explore, and she has videos, books, and presentations that can help us all become better at providing the deep understanding that our students deserve.

In a K-U-D, the understandings contain the big ideas of the unit, but more importantly, they are ideas that transcend it and apply to a variety of content. Think of them as thesis statements, and the *knows* are the content-specific ways in which you would prove these statements.

*Understanding*s should be engaging but not gimmicky, general enough to apply to lots of content but specific enough to be relevant, and true without being factual. They should be important and conceptually sticky, meaning that they apply to lots of facts and knowledge, not only a specific set. As Carol Tomlinson said in a conference once, these are the "goose bump" parts, the enduring truths that help us understand the world a little bit better. Understandings are really difficult to craft, as you are trying to capture the essence of the learning in a single, concise sentence. We would often draft a bunch, then spend hours arguing over the wording, the truth, or the specificity, ultimately cutting down our list to two to four understandings per unit that we could agree upon. It often wasn't until after the unit was over that we could really test their effectiveness, sometimes by having students prove the understandings with the unit content (formally through a summative assessment or informally through a Socratic discussion or class activity) and other times through our reflection.

Understandings should complete the sentence starter, "By the end of this period of learning, students will understand that ..." The *that* will ensure a complete sentence. Understandings should not be *how to* statements, and using the sentence starter prevents this common practice (anything that starts with *how to* is either an activity or a skill).

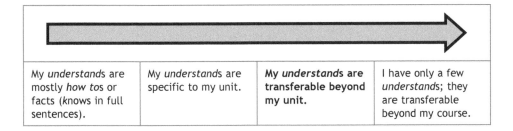

My *understands* are mostly *how tos* or facts (knows in full sentences).	My *understands* are specific to my unit.	**My *understands* are transferable beyond my unit.**	I have only a few *understands*; they are transferable beyond my course.

DOS

The *dos* are the skills that you will instruct, practice, and assess multiple times throughout the unit. They are not activities or specific assessments, and they are not skills that you plan to assess but not instruct or practice. In other words, your *dos* are your learning targets! In a standards-based class, having the *dos* be the same as the learning targets makes planning, instructing, and assessing much easier.

When we first started using K-U-Ds, we listed everything students were going to do in the *D* column. We included our assessments ("Write a persuasive essay about . . ."), our activities, ("Create a time line that connects the novel to the historical era"), and even the types of questions we had on tests ("Identify the causes of the revolution"). The *D* column was long and impressive looking but did little to keep us focused on what was most essential. Once we began the shift to SBL, the connection between the learning targets and the *D*s became obvious and provided not only focus but also efficiency. We began to see the assessments and activities as vehicles for the demonstration of vital, transferable skills, so we removed them from the K-U-D and replaced them with the skills themselves. Instead of "Create a time line" (an activity), we added "Analyze cause and effect" (a transferable skill); while we would still use the time line to demonstrate the skill, we realized that we had been obscuring what was most important. By putting the skill at the center rather than the activity, we were more able to differentiate, to provide multiple opportunities to practice, and, ultimately, to help students see the transferability of what they were learning in our class.

Because we will go into learning targets in depth in the next chapter, we are going to keep this short and sweet. Trust us here: Make the *dos* equal the learning targets and the rest will fall into place.

K-U-D EXAMPLES

Figures 1.1, 1.2, and 1.3 on the following pages show examples of K-U-Ds.

Science

FIGURE 1.1   Science K-U-D

Integrated Environmental 2015–2016 K-U-D and Scales		
Lake Champlain Unit, Part I: Ecosystems—Cycling Between Abiotic and Biotic Systems		
Know: At the end of this unit, students will know . . .	**Understand:** At the end of this unit, students will understand that . . .	**Do:** At the end of this unit, students will be able to . . .
carrying capacity. (LS2-1) biodiversity. (LS2-2) cycling of carbon, water, nitrogen, and phosphorus. No transformations. (LS2-3, ESS2-6) trophic pyramid and bioaccumulation. (LS2-4) photo/cell resp. basics. (LS2-5) abiotic and biotic factors. (LS2-1)	Earth is a complex and dynamic set of interconnected systems that interact on a wide range of temporal and spatial scales. (ESS2 Framework, pg. 179) ecosystems are complex interactive systems that include both biological communities and physical components of the environment. (LS2 Framework, pg. 150) changes of energy and matter in a system can be described in terms of flows into, out of, and within that system. (PS3-3 Crosscutting Concepts)	create a clear, accurate model that represents basic and complex relationships between components. select and use vivid, relevant evidence to define a relationship. highlight text that supports the purpose for the reading prompt and use the margins to show in-depth understanding by explaining how the highlighted text supports the purpose for reading.

Math

FIGURE 1.2   Math K-U-D

Trigonometry and Precalculus		
Know: By the end of the year, students will know . . .	**Understand:** By the end of the year, students will understand that . . .	**Do:** By the end of the year, students will be able to . . .
trigonometric, polar, parametric, polynomial, exponential, power, and logarithmic relationships. explicit, implicit, and parametric equations and formulas, with appropriate vocabulary and notation. strategies for solving equations and using formulas to answer questions and make predictions. technology tools for visualization, investigation, and verification.	families of relations and functions have similar characteristics. mathematical operations manipulating x and y result in graph transformations. equations and formulas describe mathematical relationships.	interpret graphs to answer questions or make predictions. evaluate equations or formulas for specific values to answer questions or make predictions. convert between rectangular, polar, and parametric forms for mathematical relationships. model a data set with the appropriate relation or function both graphically and algebraically. use mathematical models to make predictions from data.

Created in collaboration with Monica Carter.

FIGURE 1.3 Humanities K-U-D

Cycle 2: September 21–November 6ish		
Exploration and Morality		
You got blood on your face, you big disgrace, wavin' your banner all over the place.		
Know: At the end of this cycle, students will know . . .	**Understand:** At the end of this cycle, students will understand that . . .	**Do:** At the end of this cycle, students will be able to . . .

essential geographical elements and places.
 	
the impact of Mongol exploration and choices on Europe.
 	
the impact of the travels of Marco Polo.
 	
the impact of guns, germs, and steel.
 	
the motivations for and impacts of European exploration.
 	
details about Pizarro's conquest of the Incan civilization.
 	
significant inventions and innovations of the time period.
 	
Texts:
 	
   Choice Reading.
 	
   Excerpts from journals, novels, textbooks, primary documents, and other applicable texts.
 	
   Selected TED Talks, movie clips, and other applicable videos.
	geography may be the single greatest determinant of a civilization's success or failure.
	
	necessity is the mother of invention.
	
	there are moral implications to exploration and progress.
	
	a connected world leads to great progress and great destruction.
		determine the type of reading or note-taking strategies that should be used based on the purpose of the reading or assignment.
		
		determine the big ideas within a text.
		
		support ideas with multiple pieces of evidence.
		
		show relationships between and among elements of specific historical periods, topics, or units of study, including cause and effect.
		
		graphically represent ideas.

Challenges

Time for Creation and Reflection: Creating and reflecting on K-U-Ds isn't easy, so one of the biggest challenges is making time to thoughtfully create documents that can drive the learning. Creating a K-U-D forces us to really think about and commit to answering the question, "What do we want our students to be like at the end of this unit or class?" At first glance, this may seem like a simple question, but the complexity comes when we need to honestly evaluate whether our class supports this goal. The K-U-D can force this internal discussion. If we write K-U-Ds in order to prove to an outside audience that we are covering certain content or addressing certain state or national standards, however, then we have wasted time. These documents need to be used in our daily practice and need to be useful to us at the classroom level. To be most effective, they should be given to students at the beginning of learning, returned to often throughout the unit to check for learning, and then evaluated at the end of the learning for accuracy and effectiveness. Having students help us revise the K-U-Ds is the ideal, but this takes time as well.

Conflict With Current Systems: In addition to the extra time, some teachers or administrators may challenge the need for the K-U-D as a curriculum-planning document, and technically, they are right. Unlike targets and scales, which are essential to a standards-based classroom, the K-U-D is one of many types of curriculum documents that can help us determine the *what* and *why* of our choices, and teachers and schools often have a different favorite format or mapping system. But the simplicity and clarity of the K-U-D beautifully supports the complexity of what follows, so we included it here as a strong suggestion. When working with teachers new to SBL, the K-U-D can make the overwhelming seem reasonable; having a single document that frames the unit brings simplicity to the complex changes necessary for SBL and sets us up for success. We would not be where we are today without it.

The Guilt-Free Box

Overwhelmed by the thought of creating K-U-Ds for all of your units? Confused by the differences between the *K*s, *U*s, and *D*s? That's okay. It took us years to get our K-U-Ds in a place we were happy with for a single course, so start small.

Consider these starting points:

- Cut yourself some slack on your K-U-Ds. It's okay to end up with bad ones for a while. We did this for years, and it actually helped us figure out how to write effective K-U-Ds. Even a bad K-U-D will help you figure out your intentions for your students. No need to share them with anyone at first; just keep them in the front of your planning book and make changes and revisions as you go through each unit. They will get better.

- Skip the *U*s at first. Enter your *K*s and *D*s, and then add understandings as you figure them out. Or, conversely, start with only the *U*s and add the others as you go.

CHAPTER 2

Creating Learning Targets

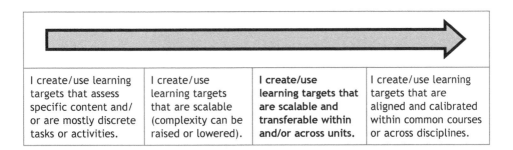

I create/use learning targets that assess specific content and/or are mostly discrete tasks or activities.	I create/use learning targets that are scalable (complexity can be raised or lowered).	**I create/use learning targets that are scalable and transferable within and/or across units.**	I create/use learning targets that are aligned and calibrated within common courses or across disciplines.

COMMENTARY AND CONTEXT

One of the most frustrating trips I ever took was to see a college friend in Boston one summer. It was 1990, and she left a message on my home answering machine just before I left and told me to drive south and follow the signs as I went. She told me to call when I got there and she'd give me her address. Being a bit smarter than that, I found an old map in my father's car, circled Boston, and was on my way. Knowing I was headed to the city was helpful for a while, but it turns out, there are a lot of exits for Boston. And there were no cell phones. So, after a frustrating two hours of pay phones, busy signals, and a ridiculous number of one-way streets, I arrived wishing I hadn't even started the journey.

Now that I have GPS, I can't even imagine what it's like not to have a clear destination. GPS (and cell phones) have increased our efficiency, improved our accuracy, and allowed many of us to get to places we never thought possible.

That's what learning targets do. They provide clear, specific skill destinations and give students the confidence they need to start the journey. Scales (which we'll talk about in the next chapter) provide the route.

Many of you may be a part of a professional learning community (PLC) at your school. If so, it's probably closely aligned with the work of Richard DuFour. He wrote about the four essential questions for PLCs, and the learning target is central to them all (DuFour & Eaker, 1998).

1. What is it we want our students to learn?

2. How will we know if each student is learning each of the skills we have deemed most essential?

3. What will we do if they don't learn it?

4. What if they already know it?

Learning targets are the answer to the first question—What is it we want our students to learn?—and they drive all of the others. They clearly articulate what the learning looks like, allowing teachers to more efficiently and intentionally design instruction, assessment, and opportunities for relearning or new learning. They also allow students to see what they're aiming for. Students can hit any target they can see and that stands still for them, which means that our first job as teachers is to firmly plant these targets in their line of sight.

There are many definitions of the term *learning target* in play in education right now. Imagine being an American in a bar in London. The guy next to you asks if you saw last night's football game. You respond with excitement about the Pittsburgh Steelers' game-winning drive as he starts to excitedly tell you about Liverpool's dramatic comeback victory over Manchester United. You are both talking about football, but *football* means something completely different to each of you, so it will quickly become frustrating if you don't clear this up.

In order to prevent an awkward bar conversation here, we are going to clearly define our use of the term *learning target*. We understand that many of you may be working in a system that defines the term differently, so please be sure to take that into consideration when reading this chapter and beyond. *Learning targets* as we define them are not the same as *standards*. Standards are broader, often more general destinations that drive our decisions about curriculum. While these standards (Common Core State Standards [CCSS], Next Generation Science Standards, National Health Standards, etc.) can provide direction, they are often not very helpful (for us or for students) when it comes to specific instructional design and assessment. Learning targets, in contrast, are more precise. They come from breaking down (or unpacking) standards into the context of our learning experiences, providing more specific destinations for learning within our units or classes.

Now is a good time to tell you our philosophy about learning targets, and you can certainly find examples and experts with conflicting beliefs and definitions. We will define a few different types in The Practical Part (to follow), but first, we're going to explain why we landed on our model. When we first started looking at learning targets years ago, we went to conferences, bought books, and then started visiting schools around New England. We were looking for a model that matched our district's beliefs about learning. Everywhere we went, we saw content targets. In some places, these targets allowed for limited choice in content, but mostly we saw long checklists (of course) and discipline-based content targets. And because the focus of the targets was content, the overwhelming focus in the class-rooms we visited was content. We saw lots of textbooks and worksheets (paper and digital), lots of multiple-choice quizzes and tests, and lots of teachers at the front of the classrooms. In some places, students knew exactly what target they were trying to hit and in others, they were less clear, but in all, they were focused primarily on knowing, not doing.

The schools we visited may have been extreme, but the patterns we saw made us nervous. Our mission statement was about getting students to think critically, solve problems, and transfer learning, and we hadn't seen much of that. We saw compliant students who were following directions, moving from task to task, and checking off learning (sometimes literally on wall charts). When they met a target, they moved to another end of learning. It was unclear whether their competency in these targets would transfer beyond the walls of their classrooms.

We quickly began looking around for other models and soon came across pockets of educators around the country who were using transferable skill targets instead of specific content-based targets. These targets allowed students to demonstrate their proficiency using rich, varied content—sometimes chosen by the teacher and sometimes not—and allowed teachers to return to essential and transferable skills throughout the year.

Our belief about targets is not shared by all, but from our experience and that of many of the teachers we work with, focusing on skill-based learning targets leads to much deeper knowledge about our content. We give some examples in the next section that will help illustrate our approach and the outcome.

THE PRACTICAL PART

Whether you are in a school that is using national standards or a system driven by internally developed standards, it's always good to start with the end in mind. So, when writing learning targets, start with the standards. What will your target help students become better at? What skill are you intentionally trying to build in order to ensure that students eventually reach the larger standards?

In our district, we have a set of 14 academic standards that drive learning and that will determine graduation proficiency at the end of the K–12 experience. They were developed internally over multiple years, were guided by state and national standards, and are regularly reviewed and revised as we learn more about learning. Similar to our learning targets, these standards are *transferable*, meaning that they are not organized by discipline areas but can apply to all disciplines. All of the learning targets in our district are written to provide evidence of one of these standards, allowing students to build their skills over time and across disciplines.

CHAMPLAIN VALLEY SCHOOL DISTRICT: PROFICIENCY-BASED GRADUATION STANDARDS
CREATIVE AND PRACTICAL PROBLEM SOLVING
a. Generate a variety of solutions, supported by evidence.
b. Interpret information and derive meaning through the use of inference, empathy, metaphor, or imagination.
c. Frame questions, make predictions, experiment with possibility, and design strategies.
d. Develop and use generalizations, models, or abstractions.
e. Set goals, make informed decisions, and take constructive risks.
CLEAR AND EFFECTIVE COMMUNICATION
a. Understand and use discipline-specific vocabulary.
b. Demonstrate organized and purposeful communication.
c. Adjust communication to suit the purpose, context, and audience.
d. Demonstrate standard conventions of expression, including oral, written, performed, and emerging technologies.
e. Participate and collaborate effectively and respectfully to enhance the learning environment.
INFORMED AND INTEGRATIVE THINKING
a. Use evidence and reasoning to effectively support ideas or solutions.
b. Identify main and supporting ideas, patterns, trends, clues, and relationships in sources of information.
c. Analyze, evaluate, and synthesize information and perspectives to build understanding.
d. Evaluate the accuracy, bias, and usefulness of information.

There are so many great books, online resources, and workshops to help you move from standard to target, often known as *deconstructing standards*, *unpacking standards*, or *unwrapping standards*. Google any of these terms and you will find clear, step-by-step processes to help break the standards into targets. The work of Rick Stiggins has been particularly helpful to many of our teachers (see Further Exploration for specifics), and we highly recommend looking closely at his strategies and systems. We are not going to focus on the move from standard to target but will instead look closely at the elements of effective targets themselves.

If you are anything like us, you will start with way too many targets, and they will either be too vague or too specific. We encourage you to experiment and not get too caught up initially in perfection, as the only way to really know if targets are effective is to use them with real, live students. We also encourage you to collaborate during this process. Ultimately, we need our targets to be calibrated and common among courses so that our assessment is as accurate as possible and our evidence has integrity; this calibration takes time, however, so if you wait for complete agreement and alignment, you may never actually use the targets.

As you saw in the previous chapter, we streamlined the process by making our *dos* (from the K-U-D [know, understand, do]) the learning targets. Here, we will go into more depth about what makes a successful target and what to avoid. As you know, we have a very particular approach to targets that may differ from other schools', so for the sake of clarity, here are a few rules we are playing by when writing targets: the *scope* of our targets must be appropriate to a reportable period of learning (a unit or a trimester), they must be *transferable* (meaning not limited to a single piece of content or activity), and they must be *scalable* (able to be ratcheted up or down in skill complexity). We will discuss the first two of these rules in this chapter and the third (scalable) in the next chapter.

SCOPE

How we write our targets can determine the scope of the learning we expect. Targets are different than standards in that they are intentionally written to provide achievable goals over a reasonable amount of time. Learners need to be able to see progress on a skill in order to persevere through difficult learning, so we must establish goals that can be met within a particular unit and provide concrete steps on the way to and beyond the goal (see the section on scales in the next chapter). When students see progress, they are more likely to stick with the learning, even when it gets difficult. Making sure our targets are set to the appropriate scope provides the motivation necessary to continue pushing toward more rigorous learning. This is particularly important in systems that still require grades at the end of marking periods; it is not fair to students to grade each quarter on a yearlong target. If we have to translate learning to a grade, then the grade must be based on achievable targets that have scopes that match our reporting periods.

Here are three of the most common scopes (some teachers call them *grain-sizes*) we see in our schools:

- **Yearlong:** A yearlong target is a target the teacher anticipates will take the entire year for students to become proficient in. While this is fine in theory, we need to break these down into more incremental learning goals that we can track and report. Yearlong targets can be broken into unit or reporting period targets, either by breaking the target into parts or by looking at expected progress and recalibrating your goals. Students (actually, all humans) need to see growth in order to stick with learning, so when writing targets, we must determine the appropriate level of achievement in the skill over a smaller period of time. If we are scoring using a 1-4 scale, it's difficult to report 1s and 2s all year and expect students and parents to understand that learning is happening; in addition, these scores are too broad to be useful to us as teachers when we are trying to respond to our data in order to differentiate. Think of training for a marathon, where the goal (target) is to run 26.2 miles. For the first six weeks of training (in an 18-week program), the runner cannot be expected to run the full 26.2 miles; her six-week target might be 10 miles, so her distance achievement at that time should be based on the appropriate expectation. Thus, she would be scored on her achievement of the Week 6 goal at that time, not the Week 18 goal. This is the same for learning. It may be easier to think of yearlong targets as standards that need to be broken into parts or shifted into incremental chunks or more targeted targets. These are more precise and specific and provide smaller destinations—where students should be along the way in order to be prepared to meet the yearlong standard.

    Example of Yearlong Target: Note the number of parts in this target; it may not be realistic to expect students to be proficient in all parts of this target early in the year, so breaking it into achievable parts and then writing scales will help us instruct and provide feedback.

I establish and maintain a clear purpose in my writing through a thesis and leads, the choices I make in the body, and my conclusion; my purpose is appropriate to my audience and to the assignment and stays consistent throughout my writing.

- **Repeating:** A repeating target is a target that will repeat in multiple units or over multiple reporting periods, and the teacher anticipates that most students will reach proficiency each time with different content. This is the most common type of transferable target, often being introduced and heavily instructed in an early unit and then brought back throughout the year. For example, targets that ask students to show cause and effect, that ask students to make claims, or that ask students to create models would all be targets that could repeat over and over with new (and perhaps more complex) content.

    Example of Repeating Target: Note that this target will be instructed, practiced, and assessed in multiple units with different content; in later units, more time can be put on the practice, as instruction will be much more targeted, based on need.

I have a clear claim with multiple relational ideas; the claim requires varied evidence and substantive analysis to prove.

- **Unit:** A unit target is a target that appears in only one unit or trimester and is not repeated for the full class once that unit/trimester is complete. These targets should still be transferable within the unit, meaning that they can be practiced over and over with different unit-specific content. In addition, even though the target will not formally repeat, students who did not meet proficiency should still have an opportunity to show new learning later in the year. Our job is to ensure that students learn, not only to teach, which means that unit targets may need to be readdressed for some or all of our students. If they are truly transferable, bringing them back with new content should be fairly easy.

  Example of a Unit Target: Note the specificity of this target. While it could be used with a variety of texts and levels of complexity, the intention is to address it in one unit and then move on.

I can analyze how an author uses rhetoric to advance a specific point of view or purpose in a text.

TRANSFERABILITY

We mentioned transferability a few times in the previous paragraphs, and here's what we really mean. Our targets have to allow students the opportunity to practice a skill using our content. This is how they will learn the content, so the more they can practice throughout the period of learning, the better. In order to allow this practice, targets need to be based on a transferable skill and not be anchored by content that is too specific. If our target asks students to label or identify or describe a specific part of our curriculum, they are limited in their ability to practice this with other content. For example, asking a student to identify causes of the Civil War may be essential to our course, but to what end? Is it so they learn to see the relationship between events and their multiple causes? Is it to be able to predict outcomes based on past events? If our target is "I can track the interrelationship among multiple causes of an event" or "I can analyze outcomes based on multiple causes," then we are raising the rigor and allowing students multiple opportunities to practice this skill within our class prior to the summative assessment. Another benefit of transferable targets is that we can share them among units, courses, and content areas. The more students can see that the skills we are asking them to develop are not limited to single courses, the more meaningful their learning will be.

Targets can be transferable within courses, within discipline areas, or across discipline areas—as long as they allow multiple and varied opportunities for practice. Look at the difference between transferability in the following targets for a painting and drawing class:

- **Nontransferable, Content Based:** I can use multiple and varied painting techniques in my self-portrait. (This target is specific to an assignment. Unless the student will be creating many self-portraits, this is not easy to practice.)

- **Transferable Within a Course**: I can use multiple and varied painting techniques in my artwork in a way that supports my intent. (This target can now be practiced throughout the painting unit, allowing the student to get feedback on their use of the multiple techniques along the way.)

- **Transferable Within a Discipline**: I can use multiple and varied techniques in my artwork in a way that supports my intent. (By removing the medium, this is now able to be used in other art courses. The benefit of this is greater efficiency of learning for students. When they have experienced success with a target using one set of content [or one medium], they are more likely to experience success with unfamiliar content [or media].)

- **Transferable Across Disciplines**: I can apply multiple and varied techniques in my work in order to support my purpose. (Just by changing the discipline-specific vocabulary, this target can be used in other content areas.)

The assurance we must make when using transferable skill-learning targets is that the content is still central to the learning. We should communicate our *knows* and *understands* clearly to students and parents and ensure that students are using that content to practice and demonstrate the skills in our targets.

Some Reminders About Learning Targets:

- Learning targets are classroom-level descriptions of what learning looks like for a particular standard at a particular level.

- Learning targets should help students understand what we want them to learn; they are as much for students as they are for teachers, as one of our goals is to develop learners that are self-aware.

- Learning targets can and must be instructed, practiced, assessed, tracked, and reported over time. They are not to be used only to assess.

- Learning targets are scalable. They exist within a skill continuum that we define for students (the scale).

EXAMPLES

The chart on the opposite page shows a variety of examples of learning targets in use in our district. Note that each has an achievable scope and could be used with a variety of content, some within a discipline and some across disciplines.

HUMANITIES	MATH	SCIENCE	WELLNESS	WORLD LANGUAGE	ARTS & TECHNOLOGY
I can identify multiple perspectives that impact or stem from situations.	I can write linear functions given verbal, numerical, tabular, or graphical information.	I can construct an explanation for a situation using multiple sources of evidence that are consistent with scientific ideas and theories.	I can analyze the outcomes of a decision and why they probably occurred.	I can communicate about events in the present, present progressive, and future.	I can read and perform using music notation.
I use textual evidence to support both explicit and implicit ideas.	I can apply order of operations to writing and evaluating expressions, including those with variables and exponents, when working with whole numbers.	I can create a clear, accurate model that represents basic and complex relationships between components.	I can monitor, assess, and reflect my progress toward reaching my fitness goals.	I can write Latin sentences using classical grammar, including verbs, direct objects, and prepositional phrases.	I can communicate complex ideas using digital visualizations, models, or simulations.
I can analyze how particular elements of a story change throughout the text.	I can use the distributive property to create equivalent expressions involving whole numbers and variables.	I can write a testable question that includes a clearly measurable dependent variable and a clear independent variable.	I can demonstrate appropriate sportsmanship behavior and fair play.	I can speak mostly in the target language for the designated period of time, with only minor accidental English.	I can compare and contrast the use of form and/or technique in two artworks using some content-specific vocabulary.
				I can sometimes extend conversations with comments or questions.	

Challenges

Balance: Balancing autonomy and consistency is one of the biggest challenges we faced with the creation of targets. Some schools and departments provide learning targets that all teachers must use. This certainly saves time and provides consistency in reporting, but our experience working with schools transitioning to standards-based learning (SBL) has shown that when teachers are allowed to create their own targets, they are much more likely to use these targets to change instruction—not only to assess products. This may mean that there are some early inconsistencies in the substance, quality, and number of targets, but we have found that the ownership, respect for autonomy, and understanding that comes from individual or team creation can lead to greater success and consistency in the long run. The ultimate goal is to have common, calibrated learning targets for common courses, so the more collaboration early in the process, the faster we will get to this goal.

Content Misunderstanding: Addressing the content misunderstanding is another challenge we have had, and if we could go back in time, we would spend a lot more effort to communicate this clearly. Skill-based, transferable targets should ensure greater content acquisition and deeper conceptual knowledge, but this is difficult to communicate to teachers and parents. Too often, people think of *content* and *skills* as separate and competing pieces, which couldn't be further from the truth. Content alone may help a game show contestant, but otherwise it is fairly useless. No one argues that a pilot must be able to execute landings and a doctor must be able to analyze and diagnose patients; but these are skills that cannot be separated from the content used to do them. No proponent of SBL would say that content is not important. It is vital. It is what brings the skills to life and what hooks the learner, and it is what allows us all to learn and perform with depth and transferability. The knowledge we carry on beyond our classroom walls allows us to think more deeply about issues, understand context, comprehend challenging texts, and solve problems. The difference in our approach to SBL—using skill targets instead of content targets—is that by focusing on instructing the skill, we believe we can ensure greater understanding and retention of the content we (and they) choose.

The Guilt-Free Box

Overwhelmed by the thought of writing effective learning targets? Not even sure where to begin? Wondering why someone can't give you a list of them to use?

Consider these starting points:

- Write too many targets. It's okay to overplan, and sometimes, it's actually easier at first. Remember that these will be the *D*s in your K-U-D, so it's okay if that column is long at first. When you get to the end of the unit, cross off the ones that you did not instruct, practice, and assess.

- Use someone else's targets to start. Google *skill targets* or other similar key terms. Go to #sblchat on Twitter or the Facebook group Standards-Based Learning and Grading and ask if there is someone who teaches the same course you do. There will be, and they will share their targets. It's really a lovely, generous community. As you use them, you will make changes and revisions based on your context and your learners, but it will give you a place to start.

CHAPTER 3

Building Learning Scales

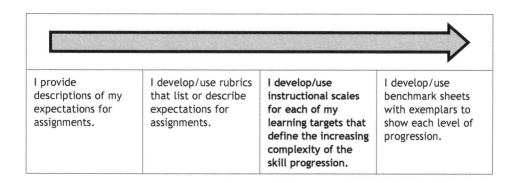

I provide descriptions of my expectations for assignments.	I develop/use rubrics that list or describe expectations for assignments.	**I develop/use instructional scales for each of my learning targets that define the increasing complexity of the skill progression.**	I develop/use benchmark sheets with exemplars to show each level of progression.

COMMENTARY AND CONTEXT

Learning scales have simplified our lives.

Scales are technically rubrics, but in order to really understand their power, we suggest you think of them as an entirely different tool at first. A *scale* is a skill progression that includes the learning target. Some schools have the target farthest to the right (as the highest level of achievement), but we chose to have the target live in the third position from the left so that there are always steps leading up to and moving beyond the target. We will talk more about that "beyond" step (which we call the *4*) in a little while.

There are significant differences between the traditional rubrics we used to use and our current instructional scales. Our old rubrics were primarily for assessment purposes; we would hand them out at the beginning of the unit (usually), but they were really there to help us grade work at the end of the learning. Scales, however, are designed to guide instruction and provide feedback along the way as well as assess achievement at the end. Scales show the continuum of learning, describing what achievement of the skill looks like at varying levels of complexity; our rubrics often showed expectations for a particular assessment, listing required components for success and pointing out that these components are missing at the levels below success. Scales allow for the development of multiple activities, practice, and assessments at each of the defined levels; our rubrics were often limited to a single assignment, with feedback on the success or lack of success on that assignment. Finally, scales use positive *I can*–type language; our rubrics usually used negative, deficit-based language.

Here's a rubric we used for years with our students, followed by a scale we now use for a similar skill:

Old Rubric for Evidence

Uh-Oh (0%-69%)	Needs Some Work (70%-79%)	Very Good (80%-89%)	Excellent Work! (90%-100%)
There is little to no evidence in this essay. It's not clear the student has read the novel.	The essay is missing some evidence or the evidence doesn't support the thesis. Evidence is not cited.	Evidence from the novel supports the thesis but isn't the best available. There are at least three pieces of evidence. Evidence is cited.	Evidence from the novel is well chosen and is clearly the best available. There are more than four pieces of evidence. Evidence is cited correctly.

New Scale for Evidence

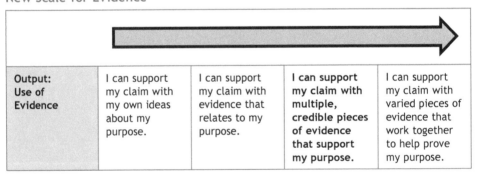

Output: Use of Evidence	I can support my claim with my own ideas about my purpose.	I can support my claim with evidence that relates to my purpose.	I can support my claim with multiple, credible pieces of evidence that support my purpose.	I can support my claim with varied pieces of evidence that work together to help prove my purpose.

There were quite a few things wrong with our old evidence rubric (Did we really have a category called "Uh-Oh"?), but the most relevant differences between then and now have to do with the language in the boxes. While the rubric at first seems more specific in the top two levels, these requirements can be provided in a checklist accompanying the specific assignment and do not need to be included in the scale itself. The language describing success is vague and subjective ("best available" and "well-chosen"). In addition, note the negative language in the first two levels—rather than point out what a beginning student can do, it documents what's missing. This may be helpful for grading, but it is not at all helpful when trying to figure out how to improve on the skill itself. If we want students to see learning as a progression, then they need to see each step as a success on the way to the next, not as a deficit to the ultimate goal. The new evidence scale, in contrast, provides a clear progression of the skill of using evidence, and when accompanied by benchmarks (see Chapter 7), it makes expectations clear and learning positive.

Just to be clear, good rubrics are scales. Our old rubrics were not good rubrics, and in order to break ourselves of ineffective habits, we found that rebranding the tool and changing the name allowed us to change our practices more successfully.

An effective scale can really be the lynchpin of a successful standards-based classroom. At the beginning of a unit, we introduce our scales, designing high-engagement, low-risk activities that allow students to reach each progressing level of the skill. Students know what's expected and know what success will feel like, so they are more likely to reach the higher levels of learning when we begin working with complex, relevant content. Throughout the learning, we use the scales to design practice activities and formative assessments, provide feedback, and plan appropriately rigorous differentiated instruction. Students use the scales throughout the learning to self-monitor and provide feedback to their peers. When it's time for the summative assessment, students use the scales to guide their work and to self-assess, and we use them to assess and communicate learning. For students who need to relearn or reassess, the scales offer feedback and direction.

In other words, scales are everywhere in a standards-based classroom; once we have developed the scales, we—and our students—have everything we need to instruct, practice, assess, and report the learning.

THE PRACTICAL PART

All levels of a scale are worded in language that shows what students can do, not what they can't do. This is not an everybody-gets-a-trophy feel-good philosophy. Learning happens on a continuum—skills grow and continue to improve over time and with practice, and when students see that learning is a progression (not a got-it-or-didn't), they are more likely to stick with it when it gets difficult. This is where the *I can* language comes in. Each box on the scale is a target for at least one of our students at any given time. If a student is currently at a 2 on our scale, then the 3 is what they are hoping to be able to do next. If they are at a 3, then they are shooting for the 4 (or whatever symbols/language you are using for your scales). That means that each box needs to clearly establish what learning looks like at that level, not what it doesn't look like.

At the top of the next page is an example of a scale we used in our tenth-grade heterogeneous humanities course. Our target skill is the analysis of relationships, an important skill that crosses disciplines and grade levels. Surrounding the target, which is in bold, we have ratcheted up and down the complexity of this skill, providing steps leading up to and beyond the target itself.

Critical Thinking: Relationships	I can explain and define individual elements within specific historical periods, topics, or units of study.	I can show understanding of one-to-one relationships between elements of specific historical periods, topics, or units of study.	**I can analyze multiple relationships between and among elements of specific historical periods, topics, or units of study.**	I can evaluate relationships between and among elements of specific historical time periods, topics, or units of study, including how these relationships inform larger ideas.

We want students to see learning as a progression, not something that you either get or don't get. As we know from Carol Dweck's (2016) work, student mindset plays a much larger role in learning than much of what we do in class; if they believe they can improve and if they see learning as the result of hard work, students are much more likely to dig in and make large gains. Think of the scales as a staircase, and each step is an achievement on its own, leading us to the next step. These steps allow students to experience success at each level and reinforce the effectiveness of the growth mindset.

There is a tendency to want to pack content details or expectations into each level in order to be clear to students, but that's not the role of the scale. We suggest using checklists or task sheets (see Chapter 6) to provide the specific expectations you have for the activity or assessment and keeping the scale simple and transferable. We want students to understand that the skills they are learning are not specific to a single assignment or essay or project or even unit, so by keeping the scales transferable, they are more likely to be able to carry their learning forward into unfamiliar and unstructured situations.

Instructional scales not only help students know what learning looks like, but they also help us differentiate more effectively, as we can design learning opportunities that allow students to practice at a variety of levels. We know that students learn best when working in their zones of proximal development, and scales help teachers and students plan for the variety of readiness levels in our classes by defining a continuum of learning. The levels on the scale ratchet up or down the complexity of the same central skill. When writing scales, it can be helpful to start at the top of the staircase and articulate the learning you hope for. Then ask, what if students attempted to do this but were unable to do it yet? What would their attempt look like? In other words, what could they do before they are able to fully achieve the top level? If each level of the scale asks for a significantly different skill, then it is really difficult to show learning as a progression or to assess multiple levels using a single assessment, so keep the central skill consistent.

HINTS AND SUGGESTIONS FOR SCALE WRITING

Pay close attention to the level 4 (the top level in your scale): In 1964, Supreme Court Justice Potter Stewart famously remarked that while he could not define *pornography*, he knew it when he saw it. We cannot take this same approach to learning. Excellence and rigor are too important to be left to chance or a student's ability to read our minds. "Wow me" is not fair to our learners. It says more about the teacher than the student and, most importantly, does not at all support what we know about learning. It is unfair to require students to go above and beyond what we intend them to learn in our classes in order to achieve the highest level (particularly if this is all going to be translated into a grade). So, we must carefully and intentionally articulate what achievement of the skill looks like at this highest level and then objectively score student work against that articulation. It's not okay to tell students or parents that you don't give 4s or that you save the 4 for the work that blows you away; our ultimate goal should be to get all students to the highest level of learning, and by clearly defining that level and providing benchmarks, we are much more likely to be successful with that goal. There are many other ways teachers can celebrate work that blows them away or stands out from the rest of the class. An e-mail or phone call home, a personal note asking the student for permission to keep their work as an exemplar, or a photo in the school paper can all honor "wow me" moments much more fairly and effectively than a score.

Another reason to pay attention to the 4 is that students and parents will. If you are new to standards-based learning, students and parents will still be equating your scoring system to the traditional grading system, so they will see the 4 as an *A* (particularly if you are still required to convert to letter grades). Making that *A* ambiguous or unreachable virtually guarantees that you will spend the majority of your time defending questionable practices that are "preventing Jessie from getting into Yale." Many students and parents are motivated to get the highest score possible, so rather than fighting that motivation, we can use it to our (and our students') advantage by clearly defining what complex, rigorous learning looks like at that highest score.

Create Benchmark Sheets: In order to be as clear and as precise as possible with your students, we suggest creating benchmark sheets and explanations to go along with the scales, and we go into much more detail about these in Chapter 7 (including examples). Creating these documents forces teachers to articulate and specify what it takes to move along the scale. This intentionality improves our ability to talk to students about skills, to provide targeted feedback, and to more intentionally design and differentiate instruction. Benchmark sheets take time, as they require experience with the scale and student work examples, so start with the scales that are most important to your course or that will repeat throughout the year.

Lose the Numbers (or Symbols or Words): As we transition away from traditional grading practices, it can be helpful to avoid any shorthand way of identifying achievement when communicating with students during the learning process. Most of us work in systems where we will need to use numbers (1–4) or words (beginner, practitioner, etc.) to represent learning, but if we can avoid this during the feedback and learning process, we can help students see the skills behind the notations. The scales can work as narrative feedback as long as students aren't constantly translating them into numbers and seeing them as judgement; this takes time and practice, but eventually, students will start to use the language within the scale to ask questions and assess their work. We can help with this by requiring such questioning. Instead of "How do I get a 4 on this?" or "Why did I get a 2?" students will begin to ask, "How can I find more varied evidence?" and "I need more relevant evidence to build a stronger argument. Can you help me figure out how to do this?" These questions show understanding of the skill behind the numbers, changing the motivation from numbers or letters to skill improvement.

EXAMPLES

Middle School Multidiscipline Scale

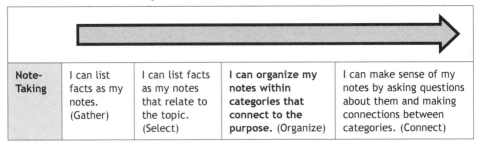

Note-Taking	I can list facts as my notes. (Gather)	I can list facts as my notes that relate to the topic. (Select)	**I can organize my notes within categories that connect to the purpose.** (Organize)	I can make sense of my notes by asking questions about them and making connections between categories. (Connect)

Middle School Math Scale

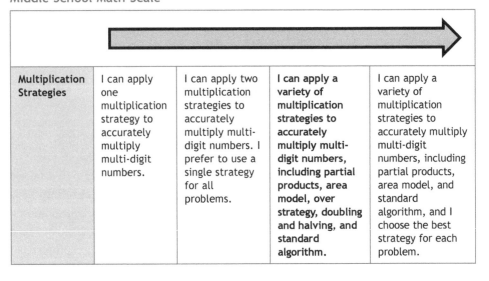

Multiplication Strategies	I can apply one multiplication strategy to accurately multiply multi-digit numbers.	I can apply two multiplication strategies to accurately multiply multi-digit numbers. I prefer to use a single strategy for all problems.	**I can apply a variety of multiplication strategies to accurately multiply multi-digit numbers, including partial products, area model, over strategy, doubling and halving, and standard algorithm.**	I can apply a variety of multiplication strategies to accurately multiply multi-digit numbers, including partial products, area model, and standard algorithm, and I choose the best strategy for each problem.

High School Science Scale

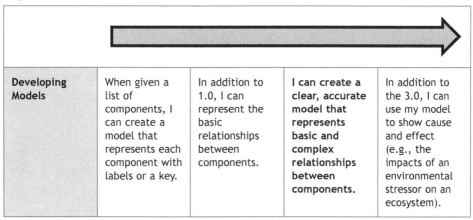

Developing Models	When given a list of components, I can create a model that represents each component with labels or a key.	In addition to 1.0, I can represent the basic relationships between components.	**I can create a clear, accurate model that represents basic and complex relationships between components.**	In addition to the 3.0, I can use my model to show cause and effect (e.g., the impacts of an environmental stressor on an ecosystem).

High School Cooking Scale

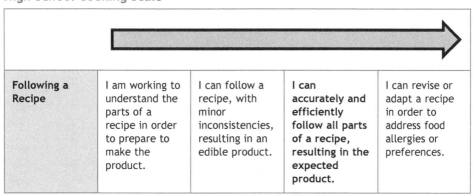

Following a Recipe	I am working to understand the parts of a recipe in order to prepare to make the product.	I can follow a recipe, with minor inconsistencies, resulting in an edible product.	**I can accurately and efficiently follow all parts of a recipe, resulting in the expected product.**	I can revise or adapt a recipe in order to address food allergies or preferences.

High School Social Studies Scale

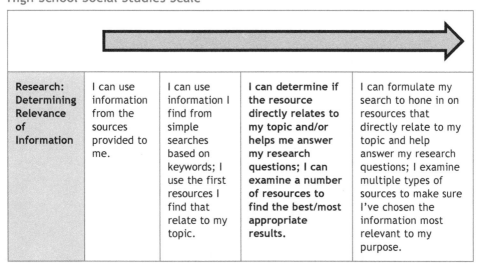

Research: Determining Relevance of Information	I can use information from the sources provided to me.	I can use information I find from simple searches based on keywords; I use the first resources I find that relate to my topic.	**I can determine if the resource directly relates to my topic and/or helps me answer my research questions; I can examine a number of resources to find the best/most appropriate results.**	I can formulate my search to hone in on resources that directly relate to my topic and help answer my research questions; I examine multiple types of sources to make sure I've chosen the information most relevant to my purpose.

Challenges

Skill Articulation: Many teachers really struggle to define what success looks like at all levels of learning. We addressed the 4 above, but the 1 can be equally challenging. It's very difficult to define early levels of learning in a skill without using negative language such as *does not*, *lacks*, or *is missing*. Because of this, teachers often turn to frequency for these early levels (*rarely*, *sometimes*, *mostly*, *always*). We suggest avoiding this trap, as it diminishes the power of the scales and makes differentiating more difficult and less respectful of the learning process. Including frequency implies that it's not the skill itself we expect improvement on, but rather, how often the student can do the skill, leading to the damaging belief that the skill is a given. If we see our role as an instructor, then we need to instruct the skill, not hope that students will become more consistent over time. Yes, there are some skills that are easy to obtain and then need to be practiced for consistency and automaticity, and we can build that important practice into our daily plans. We can even track this consistency and communicate it to students and parents, but focusing our scales on the skills that we are responsible for instructing will allow us to be more efficient and effective with our limited time.

Supported versus Independent: Another trap to avoid when writing scales is the *with support* modifier in the early levels of learning. First, if we are really challenging all students, then all students will need support at all levels, and to state otherwise undermines what we want students to understand about learning. Second, summative assessments should be independent and without support (unless there are accommodations based on a formal plan), so including the words *with support* should make us question the accuracy and legitimacy of the final assessment of achievement. Supports should happen along the way for all students, with occasional independent snapshots (formatives) to check the status of learning; these snapshots then inform the types of supports or scaffolding we need to maintain, add, or remove as we continue learning.

The Guilt-Free Box

Overwhelmed by the thought of writing scales for all of your targets? Struggling to write for all levels and ready to give up? Scales are incredibly difficult and time-consuming to create, so you may need to compromise the quality at first to prevent complete paralysis.

Consider these starting points:

- Enter your learning targets into the *3* of your blank scales template (see Appendix) and start there. After you get student work in for the first time, pile all the work that matches the target into one spot, then make piles around that. Those that do more than your expected target probably have a few things in common. Jot those things down in the 4 column. Do the same for those that don't quite meet the target. In this way, you can slowly build your scales over the length of the unit, and they will be ready to go for the next unit (or next year).

- Cut yourself some slack on the quality at first. It's okay if you can think of no other way than frequency to show the difference between levels of a skill—but if you have to do this, use *almost always*, *often*, and *rarely* rather than quantifiable percentages or numbers. Progress, not perfection, is the goal, so start where you need to start.

CHAPTER 4

Collaborating With Special Educators

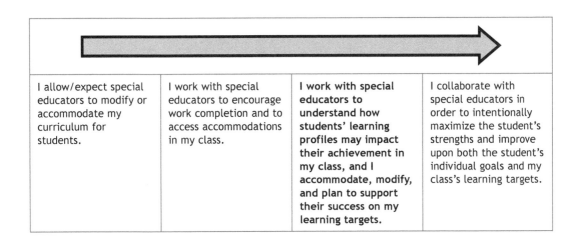

I allow/expect special educators to modify or accommodate my curriculum for students.	I work with special educators to encourage work completion and to access accommodations in my class.	**I work with special educators to understand how students' learning profiles may impact their achievement in my class, and I accommodate, modify, and plan to support their success on my learning targets.**	I collaborate with special educators in order to intentionally maximize the student's strengths and improve upon both the student's individual goals and my class's learning targets.

COMMENTARY AND CONTEXT

For the past eight years, we have been lucky enough to collaborate with two excellent special educators in our classroom, Sarah Crum and Jess Hoskins. Both Sarah and Jess taught us more about our role in student success than we could have learned from any book or in any class. Many of the team-taught courses in our school are paired with a special educator, which allowed much more consistent and effective support of our students on individual plans. Over time, many of these pairings turned into true coteaching models, where classroom teachers and special educators planned together, taught together, and looked at student work together. This was true with both Sarah and Jess in our class, and they were right beside us as we transitioned to standards-based learning (SBL). Along with their colleagues, they grappled with questions of fairness, equity, clarity, and legality.

We all read Lee Ann Jung and Thomas Guskey's (2012) work, went to conferences, and experimented with systems and structures that would help all of our students learn more effectively.

Perhaps the most important lesson Jess and Sarah taught us was that language matters. Students in our classrooms with individualized education plans (IEPs) belong to us as much as the students without plans. They are not *special ed. students* or *the special educator's students*. They are *our* students, and it is our responsibility to help them learn. The special educator has resources, information, and expertise that can help us help them—and in many cases, can help us help all of our students—but we are still the classroom teachers, and our job is to help every student in our classes maximize his or her learning. When classroom teachers talk to special educators and refer to students on a plan as *your students*, we are sending a clear message to and about the student: You are different than the rest of the class and you are not my responsibility. In addition, when we use *special education* as a modifier, as in "*she's a special ed. student* or, collectively, *our special ed. students*, we are discounting who those students are as individuals and as learners.

So, what does all this have to do with K-U-Ds (*knows*, *understands*, *dos*), targets, and scales? Well, we included this chapter here in Part I, even though there are implications for assessment, instruction, and reporting as well, because so much of our success with all students is determined by the clarity of our goals. Knowing how to work collaboratively with our special educators to accommodate or modify our targets and scales can drive the success of our students, and it can help us understand learning better.

When planning with special educators, having a K-U-D and scales for an upcoming unit can help focus on strengths rather than deficits. The special educator knows the learners on his or her caseload well, or at least understands them as learners better than we may at the beginning of a course. Jess would always ask for one copy of our K-U-D and scales for each student on her caseload, and she would schedule time to sit with us to go through the student's IEP in comparison to our scales. Together, we would anticipate areas of strength and weakness. Next to each scale, we would write one of the following notations:

- **OK:** This meant that the target and scale, as written, were appropriate for this student as long as he or she received accommodations. Often, the special educator would provide suggestions at this time of the type of accommodations that would be most successful for this skill, where the student might get stuck, and anything else that was relevant to our content or the student.

- **X:** This meant that the target and scale were not appropriate for this student. At times, Jess would suggest that we remove a certain target from the student's expectations so that the student could focus on more essential skills in and out of class. This was always case by case, and if it was an essential target for the class, we would move to the third notation.

- **M:** This meant that the target and scale were not appropriate as written but could be if modified, based on the student's plan and goals. We will go into much more detail in the next few pages about types of modification and what this can look like.

By making the time to sit with Jess before each unit began—it often took no more than 30 minutes total—we were able to work together to more effectively instruct and support all of our students. We found that many of the structures and scaffolds that Jess suggested for the students who were on her caseload were also incredibly helpful to other students in our class.

We know not every teacher or special educator will be as lucky as we were to have coteaching or co-planning time, but even if those structures aren't available, being able to provide a K-U-D and scales to any colleagues who will be assisting or supporting your students will be a step in the right direction.

A few important clarifications before getting into the practical part: Understanding the difference between *accommodations* and *modifications* is necessary before determining the appropriateness of learning targets for students with learning differences. Accommodations do not require a change in the target itself. If we accommodate, we expect that the student is able to reach or go beyond our class target as long as we provide the accommodations documented in the student's IEP. Even if a student is not on an IEP, we may choose to accommodate when the accommodation is not directly related to the target skill. For example, if our target is about using evidence and most students are gathering their evidence from text, we may decide to offer a student a different form of input, as the input is not what we are measuring.

Modifications require change to the target. If we choose to modify a learning target for a student, we are saying that even with accommodations, the student will not be able to reach the target. This may be due to a related or unrelated learning challenge. Please note that any modification of course targets should be determined by the IEP team, not only by the teacher or the special educator. Lee Ann Jung has written extensively about the difference between these two terms, and much of the work to follow is a direct result of her influence and scholarship (see Figure 4.1 on the next page).

THE PRACTICAL PART

For the practical part of this chapter, we have asked Sarah Crum—coteacher and special educator—if we can use her thinking and writing about modifying learning targets. She and her colleagues have worked hard to develop a system for our district, and she has been instrumental in our own understanding of the power of coteaching.

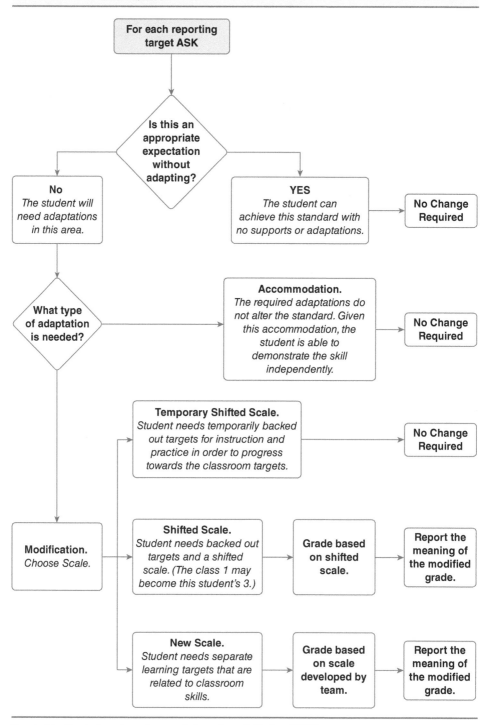

Created by Sarah Crum based on work from Jung & Guskey (2007).

Last year, we asked her to write a guest blog post for us (Crum, 2017). The next few pages are from that blog post.

We have found that the students who require modified standards generally fall into three categories: needing temporarily shifted scales, needing shifted scales, or needing new scales. However, it is important to note that students may fluctuate between categories. It is also important to note that in our experience, the percentage of students who require shifted scales or new scales is quite low: about 5% of students, five out of a grade level of 100 students, or perhaps one student in your class of twenty.

Temporarily Shifted Scale: Backing Out Targets Primarily for Instruction

This type of modification requires taking the classroom target and spending quality time articulating the 2 and the 1 as well as a couple of steps below. It helps the teacher plan for instruction, maybe breaking the learning down into smaller steps. These students may need classroom activities and tasks designed at the 2, 1, or even below to make incremental steps toward the 3. But by the end of the unit, these students can perform consistently on the typical classroom targets (may be receiving 1.5, 2, 2.5) but have clearly made significant progress in learning throughout the unit because they started at the 1 or below. These students typically feel good about their progress, and their grade is an accurate reflection of their mastery of those targets. This modification can be, and should be, used for any student who is struggling to show progress on the classroom scale. However, adding an accommodation to an IEP, 504, or educational support team (EST) plan is an important step for those students who have a plan so that communication is clear. An example accommodation is as follows: Use shifted targets to clearly define small, incremental steps in learning. This level of modification applies to the majority of mainstreamed students with disabilities (see Figure 4.2).

FIGURE 4.2 Temporarily Shifted Scale

Graduation Standard	Shifted Scale 1 Getting Started	Shifted Scale 2 Making Progress	Shifted Scale 3 (Target) I Got This!	Shifted Scale 4 I Rock This!		Classroom Target	
Writing							
Making a Claim	When given multiple sentences about the topic, I can distinguish between claims and statements.	When given a lead, I can identify the main ideas and the relationships. When given a sentence starter and word choices for the missing portions, I can complete the missing portions.	When given a sentence starter, I can complete the missing portion.	My claim is clear and contains a single idea that requires simple evidence and no analysis to prove.	My claim is clear and contains multiple ideas and requires more than one type of evidence and some analysis to prove.	My claim is complex because it contains a relationship between multiple ideas and requires more than one type of evidence and substantive analysis to prove.	My claim clearly evaluates a relationship between multiple ideas and requires a multipart system of evidence and analysis to prove.

Shifted Scale: Backing Out Targets for Instruction and Assessment

Again, this type of modification requires taking the classroom target and backing it out by articulating the 2, the 1, and below. Then the teacher assesses the student on a different set of 1-4 but uses the same targets and skills so that the ultimate goal is to get back on the classroom targets. This is a student who may start the unit two or three steps below the 1 and work toward making the 1 on the regular classroom target. This student now has a new scale: The original course target of a 1 has become this student's 3. The expected growth for the student is the same as peers in that we would hope a student would jump maybe two slots on a scale and should receive a grade that reflects that achievement (this prevents a student who has jumped from a -2, so to speak, to the 1 from receiving a D in the class when the amount of growth is the same as his or her peers). The number of targets that are backed out may vary, and depending on the student, the team can decide the appropriate credit reported; the course name can be changed on a high school transcript, if appropriate. This is the type of scenario where it may be appropriate to share the whole scale with the student and/or family (depending on the situation), so that they are clear about their child's skills in comparison to his or her peers. This can be really delicate and would be done on a case-by-case basis. The shifted scale may be incorporated into the IEP goals, but an accommodation agreed upon by the team is also included. This type of modification typically applies to students with more significant disabilities. However, it is important that the school district is willing to make this level of modification available to any student (see Figure 4.3).

FIGURE 4.3   Sample Shifted Scale

Graduation Standards	Shifted Scale 1 Getting Started	Shifted Scale 2 Making Progress	Shifted Scale 3 (Target) I Got This!	Shifted Scale 4 I Rock This!		Classroom 3 (Target) I Got This!	
Making a Claim	When given multiple sentences about the topic, I can distinguish between claims and statements.	When given a lead, I can identify the main ideas and the relationships. When given a sentence starter and word choices for the missing portions, I can complete the missing portions.	**When given a sentence starter, I can complete the missing portion.**	My claim is clear and contains a single idea that requires simple evidence and no analysis to prove.	My claim is clear and contains multiple ideas and requires more than one type of evidence and some analysis to prove.	My claim is complex because it contains a relationship between multiple ideas and requires more than one type of evidence and substantive analysis to prove.	My claim clearly evaluates a relationship between multiple ideas and requires a multipart system of evidence and analysis to prove.

New Scale: Developing Learning Goals for an Individual Student

This student is significantly below the targets in most areas and needs separate learning goals for class: new scales that may relate to the classroom targets but aren't necessarily in perfect alignment with the classroom targets. In this case, they aren't really backed out targets. The classroom teachers and special educator take data on what the student can do and develop learning goals that make sense for that student in the mainstream classroom. Because the scale is different, the course name on the transcript in high school can be different. Showing the typical classroom targets may not be appropriate here; the family may already be aware of the need for an alternate curriculum. However, it is important to communicate with the IEP team that this student needs a new scale and that this decision is made by an IEP team. This level of accommodation typically applies to students with more intensive needs, and the new scale may become some of the IEP goals for the student. It should also be listed as an accommodation for those students with a formal plan (see Figure 4.4).

FIGURE 4.4 Sample New Scale

Skill	1	2	3	4
Writing: Capacity	I can respond to a prompt in writing and sustain my writing for three minutes.	I can respond to a prompt in writing and sustain my writing for five minutes.	**I can respond to a prompt in writing and sustain my writing for 10 minutes.**	I can respond to a prompt in writing and sustain my writing for 15 minutes.
Writing: Paragraph Structure	I can write several sentences in a row.	I can write several sentences on one general topic.	**I can write a paragraph that states a general topic and includes several details on the same topic.**	I can write a paragraph that expresses a specific topic with supporting details that directly relate to that topic.
Math: Representing Numbers	When given the visual representation of a calculation with part labels, I can make connections from the parts of the visual to the expression.	When given the visual representation of a calculation, I can label the representation with the numbers.	**I can create a visual representation of the calculation (addition, subtraction, multiplication, division).**	I can create more than one visual representation of the calculation (addition, subtraction, multiplication, division).

The work that Sarah and her colleagues have done to define these modifications has been instrumental in our ability to support students. We have been able to adapt their work to support our English language learners and have unsurprisingly found that our increased facility with scaffolding strategies has led to better teaching and learning for all of our students. Having systems and structures in place to collaborate can be time-consuming at first but ultimately makes the planning more efficient.

Challenges

Planning Time: Time is once again the biggest challenge to an effective partnership between special educators and classroom teachers. We never have enough time to do everything well, but there are ways to use the time we have more effectively and creatively. First, we need to think about what we are asking our special educators and paras to do related to our classes. There should be no need to have someone in the back of the room taking notes on what the teacher says; this is a waste of time for special educators and paras. Students who need notes should get them directly from the teacher in a form that is clearly digestible and highlights the most important understandings. In addition, asking a special educator to spend time on homework support is also not a good use of time. If a student is unable to complete work outside of class independently, then it's most likely not appropriate work for that student. If the outside support is merely organizational, then finding other ways to offer that support will lead to much more efficient use of time for school personnel. Once special educators and paras are freed up from note-taking and homework support, they will have more time to collaborate and help classroom teachers meet the needs of all students.

Grading and Reporting: In a standards-based class, our scores need to communicate where students are in relation to our class targets. We cannot bump those scores up because a student tries hard or is sweet or takes longer to learn than his or her peers. Sometimes when teachers first transition away from the subjectivity of traditional grades to the objectivity of standards-based scores, students who struggle academically can suffer. In the ideal traditional school, we all graded as fairly as we could and provided appropriate instruction and practice to each of our students. In the ideal classroom, we followed all accommodations, used our students' IEPs to help guide additional instruction, and ultimately assigned grades that accurately communicated learning. But to be completely honest, that wasn't my classroom. I tried my best, but when it came time to assign grades at the end of a reporting period, I often used habits of learning scores to bring up the grades of my students on IEPs. That option goes away with SBL and standards-based grading, and often, teachers are faced with the reality that we may not be as successful with all of our learners as we pretended to be. Never before did we have to be so intentional about knowing our students' individual needs and understanding their individual goals. We were no longer able to hide behind vague grading practices, and that was terrifying. Luckily, we had a special educator who could help us figure out how to be both fair and honest, both helpful and hopeful. And before long, we were seeing incredible growth in our students and in our ability to improve their learning.

The Guilt-Free Box

Overwhelmed by the thought of modifying scales for your students? Annoyed that you don't work in a school that provides planning time for teachers and special educators? Don't panic. That's the reality for most teachers. So, start small but think important.

Consider these starting points:

- E-mail your K-U-D and scales (or only K-U-D, or only learning targets—in other words, whatever you have) to a special educator who supports one or more students in your class. Ask him or her to look at them and give you some advice. It will be the start of a beautiful relationship.

- Start being aware of the language you use when talking to your special educator about your students.

Develop Targeted Assessments

Assessment in a standards-based class is as much for the teacher as it is for the student. In fact, we would argue that for most of the year, it's more for the teacher, as assessment is what allows us to design effective instruction and ultimately improve learning. Well-designed assessments provide data that we can use within and across classes to ensure that our strategies are working and to highlight where they are not. In addition, well-designed assessments increase student engagement in their learning, as they make progress visible and demonstration of achievement authentic. Our shift to a standards-based classroom has forced us to become much more assessment literate, but we still have a long way to go; the more we understand about learning, the more we know we need to understand the assessment of learning, and so we continue to challenge past practice, experiment with new ideas, and build more effective systems. The next few chapters provide some ideas and strategies that have helped us increase the intentionality of our assessment system and improve student engagement in their assessments.

GLOSSARY OF KEY TERMS

Summative Assessment: At its core, summative assessment summarizes learning. A summative can be a specific, tangible assessment (for example, a test, an essay, or a project) or it can be a summation of previous learning (for example, determination of achievement based on a portfolio of work). Summative assessments come at the end of a period of learning (say, the end of a unit or a semester) but should not be the end of learning if the evidence shows more instruction or practice is still needed.

Formative Assessment: Formative assessment occurs during the formative period of learning, when our expectation is of growth, not ultimate achievement. Formative assessments are often quick, always targeted, and designed to determine next steps for the teacher and student. In our system, we separate formal formative assessment from practice (see next term), and formatives are intentionally designed to provide individual, in-class evidence that we can act upon in our planning.

(Continued)

(Continued)

Practice: Much of the formative period of learning for students is informal practice. Practice activities are designed to provide low-risk opportunities to play with content and skills and to allow the teacher to uncover misunderstandings, recognized patterns, and determine full-class instructional needs.

FURTHER EXPLORATION

Rick Stiggins: Rick Stiggins is one of our go-to assessment gurus. He is active on Twitter (@rstiggins) and has many excellent books on assessment that go well beyond summative assessment alone. While browsing his titles will no doubt be your best bet, we would suggest including *Balanced Assessment Systems: Leadership, Quality, and the Role of Classroom Assessment* coauthored by Carol Commodore, Rick Stiggins, and Steve Chappuis (2017) and *The Perfect Assessment System* (2017). These books can really help you to see how all the parts of assessment work together to help improve learning.

W. James Popham: Besides being one of the funniest and smartest presenters we have ever seen, James Popham's work around assessment should be required reading for all educators. If you are interested in larger questions about evaluation, accountability, and our ethical responsibilities as educators, read about the importance of assessment literacy in *The Truth About Testing: An Educator's Call to Action* (2001) or *Everything School Leaders Need to Know About Assessment* (2010). For reading more relevant to this section, definitely start with *Transformative Assessment* (2008).

Myron Dueck: We suggest *Grading Smarter, Not Harder: Assessment Strategies That Motivate Kids and Help Them Learn* (2014). This is a really fun book to read. Dueck's voice is as strong as his ideas, and he has plenty of practical examples and strategies around assessing and grading. He also has an active Twitter presence (@myrondueck) and is more than willing to help educators think about learning.

Garnet Hillman, Tom Schimmer, and Mandy Stalets: Garnet Hillman is kind of fantastic, and we credit her with surviving the early stages of our transition to standards-based learning. She started and co-moderates #sblchat and also started the Standards-Based Learning and Grading Facebook group that has provided so much support and so many ideas for teachers around the world. Her new cowritten book, *Standards-Based Learning in Action: Moving From Theory to Practice* (2018), is a wonderful, practical guide to all things standards based, but we put it in this section because of the rich content and strategies around assessment. From homework to formative assessment to feedback to summative assessment, Hillman, Schimmer, and Stalets provide exactly what teachers need.

James Nottingham: We first came across James Nottingham when someone sent us a short Vimeo clip called "The Learning Challenge." Google it for sure. It's eleven minutes long and would be great to show to students and to teachers. His explanation of the "learning pit" immediately changed the way we thought of learning, so we were excited to see that he recently published a book, *The Learning Challenge* (2017). His ideas emphasize the importance of practice and risk taking, two qualities essential to deep and lasting learning.

Buck Institute for Education: I know we don't talk much about project-based learning, but we think it's a great way to tie together many elements of standards-based learning, including authentic, engaging assessments. The Buck Institute in Northern California has been known as the gold standard for project-based learning for years now. Spending a week in Napa isn't too bad, so if you have the means and support to go to one of their weeklong institutes, we highly recommend it. But if you can't, then their book, *Setting the Standard for Project Based Learning* (Larmer, Mergendoller, & Boss, 2015), is excellent. One of the things we appreciate about the Buck Institute and this book is how grounded the work is in standards. They recognize that centering project-based learning on clear targets is the only way to ensure integrity and rigor through engaging and authentic learning experiences.

CHAPTER 5

Summatively Assessing Learning

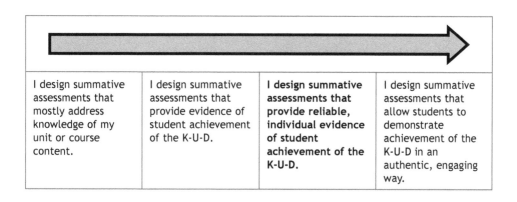

I design summative assessments that mostly address knowledge of my unit or course content.	I design summative assessments that provide evidence of student achievement of the K-U-D.	**I design summative assessments that provide reliable, individual evidence of student achievement of the K-U-D.**	I design summative assessments that allow students to demonstrate achievement of the K-U-D in an authentic, engaging way.

COMMENTARY AND CONTEXT

We know that summative assessments come at the end of a unit, but we decided to put this chapter before formative assessment and instruction because, like our students, we need to know where we are headed if we want to help students get there. We must know how we are going to assess our students' work—how we are going to determine achievement of our targets—before we can design appropriate and rigorous instruction and practice. So, we need to design our summative assessments and let our students know what they look like prior to setting out on the journey to get there.

Summative assessments are exactly as they sound: they allow students to show us what they can do with the learning, and consequently, they allow us to summarize our understanding of student achievement. They can be small, big, performance based, product based, authentic, engaging, high stakes, low stakes … in other words, there are few rules about the *what*. The only real rules are that they are intentionally and purposely designed to provide reliable, individual achievement and that they come at the end of an intentional cycle that involves instruction, practice, formative assessment, differentiation, and then more of whatever is needed to get students ready. Just because they come at the end, however, that doesn't mean summatives are the end of learning.

For years, we thought that the purpose of our summative assessments was to measure backward. In other words, we thought our summatives were tools to help us record what information students understood and could recall from the unit we were wrapping up. We asked them to look backward at the learning, and we assessed them on what we had already taught and what we hoped they had already learned. We created tests, determining the right mix of multiple-choice, short-answer, and essay questions; we designed projects that allowed choice about how students could tell us what they knew; we challenged ourselves to find new and creative ways for students to present what they had learned. All of this was great, and there were many summatives that we loved for many reasons.

Since becoming standards based, however, our thoughts on summatives have changed. While we still want students to grapple with the content and under-standings from the unit and to show us what they have already learned, what if our summatives could also extend learning? What if the end-of-unit assessments actu-ally continued the learning, requiring transfer of skills to a synthesis of new and familiar content and understandings? Once we started to think about summatives not only as a static assessment tool but as a potential vehicle for continued learning, everything changed.

The shift to transferable learning targets that drive instruction and assessment changed our summatives dramatically. We stopped focusing mostly on content and understanding and began focusing more on what students can *do* with the content and understanding. This skill focus has opened up a world of ideas about assess-ments and has helped us turn them into learning tools that extend knowledge and understanding, not just record it.

Finally, here are two things that it took us about 15 years of teaching to figure out: One, we should not be surprised by student performance on a summative. By the time we get there, we should know almost exactly how students will do (see Chapter 6 on formative assessment and practice). The summative should be a confirmation of what we know, with the stakes or the intentional design raising the achievement for many of our students. Two, we want all students to succeed. This may sound obvious, but to be completely honest, there were many times in our teaching where we thought, "Ha! This will catch them. This will teach them to blow off my homework!" Though embarrassing to admit, our summatives—particularly the tests—were often designed to reward those who had learned to play our game and punish those who hadn't. The reality is that student perfor-mance on our summatives is a direct reflection of our ability to get them to learn. If they do well, we were successful; if they do not, we weren't.

The Practical Part

There are so many ways to summatively assess, and we know that different discipline areas, different ages, different contexts, and different skills all lend themselves to different approaches. While tests may not be authentic or engaging, they (arguably) have a place in our schools. Essays, while also not always authentic or engaging, do as well. There are many great books and courses about project-based and problem-based learning, about authentic assessment and performance assessment, and we know that the inherent engagement from these types of assessment often make them superior ways to determine achievement. The key is to match our assessment method to the central skill we are assessing. If we want to assess recall, memorization, or current knowledge (the *K*s on our K-U-D [know, understand, do]), then a multiple-choice test might make sense. If, however, we are trying to assess understanding or skills in addition to the *K*s, then that method will not be the best fit. Regardless of purpose or method, all of these assessments must be intentionally designed to inspire best work, keep learning moving forward, and provide targeted and accurate evidence of current achievement.

Knowing the purpose of your assessment will help guide the design of an engaging and accurate summative. Designing it right after you create or review your K-U-D and scales will help keep this purpose central and will also help drive your formative assessments.

Here's what happens when we don't keep this purpose central to our design: A few years ago in our humanities class, we assigned a summative project about human nature and morality. We asked students to create a music video that expressed their view of the future of humanity. We had spent the unit exploring the ideas of Locke and Hobbes and reading, thinking, and writing about categorical and consequential morality. The main learning target we were assessing with the project was a critical thinking target that asked students to make connections and show relationships between and among complex ideas. We spent three weeks in class working on this summative project. At the end, we had a two-day film festival. Students loved it. We loved it. Some of the videos were funny, some were poignant, some were Oscar worthy. After congratulating ourselves for creating such an engaging summative, we sat down to assess them using our scales.

After all of the time and energy we and the students put into these videos, we were unable to accurately measure the skill we had set out to assess. There were too many clouding factors—skill with editing, filming, and sound, to name a few—and we had not intentionally designed the expectations to ensure that they would provide the evidence we needed. We ended up not being able to assess the critical thinking skill and had to develop an alternative summative in order to do so. If you think about your own past practice, projects your children have come home with, or projects you see displayed around your school, how many of them demand skills that we were not intending to measure? Are we rewarding students who can draw straight lines or who have access to incredible resources? Are we actually assessing neatness or creativity or parental skill rather than the skills or understanding we think we are assessing? Had we been clear on our purpose while designing the summative expectations, we could have ensured that the products provided the evidence we needed.

When our purpose is clear, it is much easier to design effective and engaging summatives. And engagement does not have to mean fun in the way we normally think of it. Engagement means that students lock in to the learning and try to do their best; it means they want to keep going, even when it's difficult; and it means that they are internally motivated to succeed. This is easier when our summatives are not merely asking students to parrot back learning but are requiring novel use of their learning or skills.

DESIGNING STANDARDS-BASED TESTS

When we think of tests, we think of teacher-designed assessments that all students take on the same day. They often have many items that are designed to measure how well our students know, understand, and can do what we have taught them. They are different than projects or essays or performances, though they may incorporate elements of those methods.

We strongly suggest that you design your tests from scratch when first transitioning to standards-based learning (SBL). Trying to use old, comfortable tests will lead to old, comfortable assessment practices, as many of our tests were based on the number of correct or incorrect answers, not on the skill evidence that the answers demonstrated.

When designing a test, start with the scales. Organize your test into sections (if possible, by scale and not by level within the scale). When writing questions or problems for each section, think about the student work that will come from their answers. Will this work provide evidence of achievement of the levels of the scale? Will you be able to tell definitively if they can do what the scale describes? If you imagine a completed section, how will you determine where on the scale the work falls? One suggestion we have when designing the tests is not to number your items or questions. That will help you look at each section as a collection of evidence of achievement on a particular skill.

When assessing your test, remember that you are looking at a body of evidence and comparing it to the language in your scale. As professionals, our job is to determine whether the student's work has demonstrated the skill at the target level, and if so, if it has also gone beyond (as explicitly described in your Level 4s); if not, why not? Where on the scale does the evidence fit? Assessing this way means not calculating the grade but determining the scores. This is a significant shift in thinking, and though it may initially seem to be less objective, is actually much more accurate. Consider the way many of us used to design tests. Let me tell you a few things that we did:

- Arbitrarily determined that the test would be out of 60 points rather than 100.

- Decided to make the multiple-choice section worth 25 points so that the 15 questions we had could each be worth three points and that the essay section should be worth 30 points because that's what I had left after the multiple-choice and short-answer questions.

- Decided to add a four-point extra credit question that had nothing to do with our content so that the test was worth an even amount of points.

Tests can give the impression of objectivity but are, in fact, often incredibly arbitrary. Shifting to a system where we have to determine proficiency based on an intentionally and carefully designed set of scales leads to much greater accuracy in assessment.

Last year in our humanities class, we designed a test as a summative to measure three targets (which we had instructed, practiced, and formatively assessed multiple times throughout the unit): one about note-taking strategies, one about use of evidence, and one about analyzing relationships (see sample for full scales in Figure 5.1).

The content focused mainly on the Mongols. We gave students a packet of sources about the Mongols and a complex, multipart thesis statement that they needed to prove (in class—all of our summatives are done in class only). Students broke down this thesis statement to help them organize their reading and plan their note-taking strategy. They then carefully read through the packet, taking notes and looking for evidence to help them make sense of the thesis and ultimately prove it. Then they organized their notes, rewrote, reread, and did a lot of thinking and rethinking. Next, they chose the five best pieces of evidence to prove the thesis and wrote a rationale for why they chose each piece, and why they would put the pieces of evidence in the order that they selected. In the final part of the summative, they created a mind map that connected the understandings and content from the K-U-D to what they knew and understood about the Mongols.

Here's what was different about this test: During the eight-week unit leading up to this summative, we didn't study the Mongols. We spent no time teaching about the Mongols. They spent no time learning about the Mongols. When the students got to the summative, they were faced with brand-new content. During the assessment, the students applied the skills, understandings, and knowledge we had instructed, practiced, and formatively assessed to content they had never seen before.

Figure 5.1 shows the summative in three parts.

FIGURE 5.1   Summative Assessment Example

The Mongols: The Good, the Bad, and the Ugly

Targets Assessed:

Input: Strategies	I am starting to take notes on my own when reading or listening; I list or bullet my notes; my notes help me stay on task.	I use reading or note-taking strategies that my teacher suggests. I organize my notes by source or chronologically; my choices help me remember the material.	**I determine what type of reading or note-taking strategies I need based on the purpose of the task. I organize my notes based on categories relevant to their purpose; my choices help me understand the material.**	I pick my reading or note-taking strategies based on the type of text and the purpose of the task. I organize my notes in a way that helps support my purpose; my choices help me analyze the material.
Output: Using Evidence	I can support my claim with my own ideas about my purpose.	I can support my ideas with evidence that relates to my purpose.	**I can support my ideas with multiple credible pieces of evidence that support my purpose.**	I can support my ideas with varied pieces of evidence that work together to help prove my purpose.
Critical Thinking: Relationships	I can explain and define individual elements within specific historical periods, topics, or units of study.	I can show understanding of one-to-one relationships between elements of specific historical periods, topics, or units of study.	**I can analyze multiple relationships between and among elements of specific historical periods, topics, or units of study.**	I can evaluate relationships between and among elements of specific historical time periods, topics, or units of study, including how these relationships inform larger ideas.

Part I Task:

1. Break down the thesis, which is what you are going to prove over the next two class periods—remember, you're breaking it down in order to determine what notes you need to take. This will save you time and make you more efficient.

2. Look at all the sources you have and make a plan (order, time spent on each, checkpoints for completion, etc.). You can always change it as you go, but setting some checkpoints for yourself will help make sure you can complete the task.

3. Read and take notes. Remember what you know about effective note-taking. This will take the bulk of your time.

4. Reorganize your notes in a way that helps to improve your (and our) understanding of them (and how they relate to your purpose).

Break down your thesis to help with your planning:

> **Despite their barbaric savagery, the Mongols should be remembered as civilized innovators whose ideas are still making our world a better place.**

Part II Task: Evidence: After you have finished planning, reading, note-taking, thinking, organizing, and rethinking, choose the best combination of evidence to support your thesis. You need five pieces of evidence total for this step. Please put the evidence in the order you would use if you were writing an essay.

Evidence	Rationale (why you chose it and why you put it in the order you did)	Source

Part III Task: Using one of the critical thinking map structures we have practiced in class, show the relationships between the big ideas represented in your learning about the Mongols with the *knows* and *understandings* of our unit K-U-D. You may use any of the formative or practice work you have completed in this unit. As a reminder, here is the K-U-D for your reference. Be specific, thorough, and thoughtful—show those relationships. Any supplies you need are available at the front of the room.

You got blood on your face, you big disgrace, wavin' your banner all over the place.

Know: At the end of this cycle, students will know . . .	Understand: At the end of this cycle, students will understand that . . .	Do: At the end of this cycle, students will be able to . . .
essential geographical elements and places.	geography may be the single greatest determinant of a civilization's success or failure.	determine the type of reading or note-taking strategies that should be used based on the purpose of the reading or assignment.
the impact of Mongol exploration and choices on Europe.		
the impact of the travels of Marco Polo.		
the impact of guns, germs, and steel.	necessity is the mother of invention.	determine the big ideas within a text.
the motivations for and impacts of European exploration.	there are moral implications to exploration and progress.	support ideas with multiple pieces of evidence.
details about Pizarro's conquest of the Incan civilization.	a connected world leads to great progress and great destruction.	show relationships between and among elements of specific historical periods, topics, or units of study.
significant inventions and innovations of the time period.		
Texts:		
Choice Reading.		
Excerpts from journals, novels, textbooks, primary documents, and other applicable texts.		
Selected TED Talks, movie clips, and other applicable videos.		

In previous years, we had spent days teaching about the Mongols. We told students why they were important, what they did, and how controversial they were, and on the test, they could repeat back what we had said. But the sad truth is that those past students never learned as much about or thought as much about the Mongols as the students who saw this content for the first time on the summative. If we only ask students to tell us what we told them, think what we think, know what we know, or do what we can already do, then we are preparing our students to be us. Instead, our assessments should help prepare students to encounter *new* material and *unfamiliar* ideas.

ESSAYS

When using the essay as a summative, you'll need to make a few important decisions. First, is the writing the focus of your assessment? Have you been working on skills such as thesis development, use of evidence and analysis, organization, and sentence structure? If so, then the writing is the assessment, and the content of the essay is the vehicle. If, however, your focus is on assessing critical thinking or cause and effect or a skill that is not directly related to writing, then the essay is acting as a vehicle for expressing the thinking. Second, are you allowing or requiring drafts of the essay? If yes, then how are you ensuring that you are assessing what students can do independently? If no, then are you providing enough time for students to think through and plan their ideas before writing?

Let's say the focus is on the writing and you are going through multiple drafts before getting to the final essay. Because our job when assessing is to get the most accurate snapshot of individual student achievement, we will need to summatively assess throughout the drafting process in order to ensure accuracy. For example, if you are assessing five targets with this essay (thesis, evidence, analysis, organization, and grammar/usage/mechanics), how can you be sure that a student's inability to write a quality thesis is not preventing him from choosing the best evidence? If we are assessing all five of those skills, then we need to have taught each one separately and formatively assessed them to know where students are. If we know going into the summative that a student's thesis is below target, then we also know they will be unable to excel on their evidence and analysis targets. One answer is to do the essay writing in parts. After instructing, practicing, and formatively assessing thesis writing, have students craft their thesis statements—this usually takes time, as crafting a quality thesis requires depth of knowledge and understanding of the content as well as sophisticated critical thinking in order to determine a relational argument. Once they have their thesis statements, you can summatively score these. For any students who have not reached the target on this skill, work with them to increase the complexity or craft a thesis worthy of a high-quality essay—but do not change the score for thesis writing. They have shown what they can do independently and you have documented that. But allowing them to continue to write the essay with a subpar target will limit the accuracy of the rest of your assessment. Once the thesis is set, then the students can go on to write the rest of the essay independently.

Another strategy with drafting is the "one perfect paragraph" drafting. Have students write their essays (after ensuring the thesis is sufficient). Then ask them to identify one paragraph for in-depth feedback. Spend your time solely focused on this paragraph, looking at each of the skills you are assessing and providing descriptive feedback using the scales. Allow students to revise this one paragraph as many times as they want, getting feedback on each draft as necessary. For the summative assessment of the skills, have them revise all of the other paragraphs—and use evidence from those (not the one perfect paragraph) to determine current achievement. This strategy supports what we know about feedback and the writing process but still allows us to get an accurate assessment of individual skills.

PROJECTS

Having students create, make, design, or build can be an engaging and creative way to assess targets. In some classes—art, music, tech, cooking—this is the only logical way to see what students have learned; in others—history, English, science, math—it can be an effective way to allow students to have a choice while assessing deeper understanding of content through complex skills. When designing projects or when designing criteria for choice projects, it's important to keep the scales at the center of our choices. If we are trying to assess a student's ability to predict outcomes based on patterns and trends, asking students to make multimedia time lines seems logical. But have we taught students how to use the media? Have we practiced integrating multiple forms of media to tell a story? Unless it's the use of media we are assessing, we have to make sure our expectations or student choices aren't going to get in the way of clearly assessing what we set out to assess.

When designing projects or options for projects, the most essential piece of planning is to start with the scales. Know what you are intending to assess and make that clear to students. For example, in one middle school science class we worked with, the teacher wanted students to make models of the solar system. They had been working on a modeling target, so the project made sense. She had introduced the idea to the students and let them brainstorm ideas, and they were really excited. One student was going to make a Claymation movie, two kids wanted to work together to build huge planets out of paper-mache, and another was going to bake a solar system cake. While the engagement and creativity was high, the purpose had been lost. The goal of the project was to get an accurate demonstration of each student's ability to model the solar system in a way that showed relationships and allowed predictions.

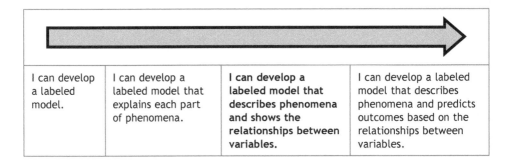

I can develop a labeled model.	I can develop a labeled model that explains each part of phenomena.	**I can develop a labeled model that describes phenomena and shows the relationships between variables.**	I can develop a labeled model that describes phenomena and predicts outcomes based on the relationships between variables.

Once the teacher brought the scale back into the planning, she realized that she was going to need to help guide the choices. Her project design could still allow choice, creativity, and student ownership, but not at the expense of demonstrating the intended learning. That didn't mean there could be no cakes or paper-mache or movies, it meant that the teacher needed to be more intentional about designing parameters and monitoring student direction. Projects have the potential to be engaging and accurately portray understanding and skills, but we need to ensure that we are being intentional and fair in our design and expectations.

PERFORMANCES

As art, drama, and music teachers already know, performance assessments and SBL are logical partners. Think about a traditional band class: the teacher sets up a clear end goal (the holiday performance) with high stakes (a real audience), provides rigorous benchmarks (professional versions of the songs they will perform), and then establishes the specific skills necessary to succeed on the goal (rhythm, accuracy, tone). The teacher differentiates based on data from formatives (tubas need more practice on "Rudolph"; French horn #2 needs to learn how to read music; violin section needs tuning), designs practices to match the upcoming summative (rehearses in the theater), and perhaps most importantly of all, hopes that all students will reach a level of excellence on the targets. SBL makes logical sense in the arts, in part because of the performance aspect of most summative assessments. We have a lot to learn from our artistic colleagues when it comes to assessments that make students try their absolute best.

Regardless of our content areas, we can replicate aspects of successful performance assessments, providing authentic audiences through TED Talks or plays, providing professional benchmarks through looking at published writing or speaking to experts in the field, providing real projects rather than simulations, and providing collaborative experiences that still require individual demonstration of skills.

MIDTERM AND FINAL EXAMS

The purpose of midterms and finals changes in a standards-based class. Rather than trying to test students on a semester or a year's worth of content, our job is to as accurately as possible determine each student's current achievement of our course learning targets and communicate that clearly to students and families. Conveniently, these exams can also provide us data to evaluate our own successes and needs. Here are a few ways standards-based teachers use exam time to ensure that they have the most accurate evidence of learning:

- **Target-Based Exams:** Some teachers want to confirm what their students know and understand through a traditional-looking test. By organizing each page (or section) of the test beneath the actual target scale, standards-based teachers are able to look at the evidence of learning in a way that is efficient and targeted. By organizing and formatting the test in this way, the expectations are clearer to students and more efficient for teachers to assess. Reorganizing tests by target also force us as teachers to be precise and intentional in our questioning. We need to think about the types of questions that will provide evidence of learning at all levels.

- **Target-Based Exams With Individual Targeted Reassessment Options:** Along with the above option, many teachers add an individual reassessment option. Teachers make the choice that *all* students will be assessed on certain targets during the exam, but once done with those, students can choose two or three more targets to reassess. Prior to this exam, teachers have made sure that students are aware of where they stand with each target so that individuals can make informed choices on what they want to reassess during this time. This has been a very effective way for teachers to ensure that they get evidence on a select number of targets, while allowing students to show improvement in areas of need and choice. Figuring out management and organization is the biggest challenge here, but teachers have come up with some great options, including color coding and personalized packets.

- **Target-Based Reflection:** Instead of giving exams, some teachers use the time to have students reflect on their achievement from the first semester. One team in our school has students going through summative portfolios (kept on a blog) that are organized by learning target. Students think about strengths, areas of growth, and challenges and ultimately set targeted goals for the second semester or the following year. This allows students to be more aware of their learning and ultimately to be more in control, while at the same time allowing teachers to gather important information about students' differences and needs. Another teacher has students write letters to their parents about their targets for their greatest strengths and needs as well as habits of learning; this letter serves as a reflection, a form of parent communication, and a writing assessment.

- **Target-Based Conferences:** In an effort to have a one-on-one discussion with students, many teachers hold target-based conferences with individuals during the traditional exam block. During these conferences, the students and teachers look at evidence of achievement of the course learning targets and collectively set learning goals for the upcoming semester. While similar to target-based reflection (above), these conferences allow dialogue about the learning. Teachers have a variety of ways to use the time for the other students, including starting work for the next semester, reflecting on work from the previous semester, or completing an independent project or exam.

One of the things we keep hearing from teachers who have transitioned to SBL and standards-based grading in their classrooms is that student anxiety around midterm assessments has gone way down. This is not because assessments have gotten easier. It's because students and teachers know prior to the assessments where they are on the targets, so the assessments become a confirmation of learning rather than something to get stressed about. There shouldn't be any surprises on midterms/finals. We, the teachers, have evidence of learning; we know what our students know, understand, and can do prior to the assessment. They, the students, have evidence of learning; they know what they know, understand, and can do prior to the assessment. That clarity of understanding makes exams feel less intimidating and more inviting.

One teacher told us last year that her class asked her to give her exam early because they were ready for it. They knew where they were because their learning had been so transparent leading up to that point. How cool is that? And it came as no surprise to the teacher that her students were right: They nailed the exam.

Challenges

Reassessment: Redoes and retakes may be necessary after a summative, and this can be challenging for teachers. How do you offer reassessment on a performance-based summative? Where do you find the time to reassess multiple students? How do you come up with another authentic way to assess? If we remember that our goal is to get accurate achievement data on a set of learning targets, then what to do about reassessment can become clearer. If a student's achievement on part of the summative does not match what you have seen during the rest of the unit, then something is wrong. Our job is to accurately communicate what a student knows, understands, and can do within the unit, so if we believe the summative scores are not accurate, then it's our responsibility to find out why. This is when a conversation, a retake, or a revision would be necessary. But we don't have to reassess everything; if we only have a question about one skill, then we find a way to get more accurate data about that skill, which may not require an entire retake.

Reassessments should also be at teacher discretion. If a student wants a do-over but her summative achievement matches her formative achievement, then a revision or retake does not make sense—we have no reason to believe (based on evidence we have seen and provided feedback on) that the student knows, understands, or can do more than the summative demonstrated, and so we would not allow a revision or retake at that time. Once new learning has occurred, however, reassessment would be appropriate and necessary.

Responsibility: One more note about reassessment. When students need to reassess, it's usually because they cannot yet do what we are asking them to do, either for skill or behavior reasons. So often in these discussions, blame or responsibility is implicitly or explicitly put on the student. If it's a skill issue, we often tell the students they need to come see us outside of class—staying after school, coming in during lunch or recess, or seeing us during a flex period—for reteaching. The clear message here is that learning happens at our pace in the classroom, and if you need more time to learn, that's on you. If we truly believe what we keep saying about learning being the constant and time the variable, then we need to stop this as a regular practice (there are always, of course, exceptions); when we have students who need reteaching—or better yet, new teaching—then we have a responsibility to shift our use of class time to address the needs of all students. Yes, this is hard and we can't always do the right thing, but if the issue is one of learning, then we must try harder to differentiate. If, on the other hand, the student needs relearning for behavioral or habit reasons, then we need to determine the source of the issue and decide what to do based on our goal, which is to help all students reach or go beyond our targets. If we know a student doesn't do homework, then assigning more homework and continuing to get mad will not help; if we know a student won't show up for extra help outside of class, allowing that student to fall further and further behind in our skills during class will not help. We need to control what we can control, and if that means having that student do something different during our class time in order to learn, then so be it. This is not to release students from responsibility, but we need to remember that they are children or young adults without fully formed frontal lobes; we, presumably, are adults. Holding them accountable to the work is the best way to teach them responsibility and, ultimately, to help them learn.

The Guilt-Free Box

Overwhelmed by the thought of changing all of your summative assessments? Worried about how much more time authentic, performance-based summatives might take? Start small.

(Continued)

(Continued)

Consider these starting points:

- Take your existing tests and reorganize them. We know we suggested starting from scratch to avoid old habits, but this is the guilt-free box, so allow yourself that step. Cut and paste your scales onto the top and then reorganize items or questions onto different pages based on similar evidence. It's a great place to start.

- Create a sane reassessment policy that supports your life outside of school. Limit reassessments to a certain day or set a "drop dead date" before the end of the quarter, after which you will no longer be able to accept work.

CHAPTER 6

Formatively Assessing Learning

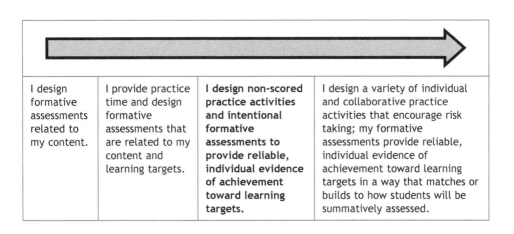

| I design formative assessments related to my content. | I provide practice time and design formative assessments that are related to my content and learning targets. | **I design non-scored practice activities and intentional formative assessments to provide reliable, individual evidence of achievement toward learning targets.** | I design a variety of individual and collaborative practice activities that encourage risk taking; my formative assessments provide reliable, individual evidence of achievement toward learning targets in a way that matches or builds to how students will be summatively assessed. |

COMMENTARY AND CONTEXT

The bulk of our time as teachers should be spent designing engaging, targeted practice for students. For most of us, this is the hardest yet most rewarding part of teaching. Though much of the literature about assessment talks about two categories (formative and summative), we have added a third (practice) in order to differentiate between a few types of formative experiences. Technically, formative assessments are practice and, technically, practice can be formative, but by separating them, we can more easily determine what and when to track achievement and how to design assessments using our scales.

We are intentionally leaving instruction out of this section but will address both direct instruction and differentiated instruction in the next few chapters. Quality teaching and learning does not have a lockstep order, and instruction and assessment become intertwined when learning is at its most efficient and effective.

PRACTICE

Learning takes time, and the best learning will require plenty of opportunities to try, fail, get feedback, and try again. That's why practice activities, assignments, and tasks need to be low risk and designed to get students to feel success at multiple levels of the scale. Students very quickly learn that it's not okay to take risks with learning when they are being scored on each attempt. When we judge their early attempts, we are showing them that we value being right, not learning. This leads to stress, low risk taking, and even cheating. Remember what it's like to learn something new—the only way to get better is to try, mess up, and try again. None of us would be able to play the guitar, ski, act, dance, read, cook, or teach if we hadn't messed up along the way; it's the same in our classes.

The idea of play is an important one during the practice phase of learning. While not everything we do in class will be fun, bringing play into the early stages can help students feel comfortable and encourage the risk taking that is necessary to learning. Allowing opportunities for social learning, group work, choice, talk, focused doodling, movement, and experimentation will increase student (and teacher!) engagement and will often highlight misunderstandings, uncover significant holes in our initial instruction, and help us identify outliers. Practice, though often the bulk of our time in class, should never be scored. The most fun we have in class is watching students practice new content and skills. When we can free ourselves and our students from the weight of assessment, great risks are taken and great learning happens. Gone should be the classrooms where we score everything students do. Let's give them space to try and fail and surprise themselves and us.

FORMATIVE ASSESSMENTS

Once students have had a chance to practice and play with the skills using our chosen content, we need to determine where they are in relation to the targets. This is when it's time for a formative assessment. Anything that is not summative is formative, as it helps form our understanding of where students are and what we need to do to help them progress; but in this chapter, we are going to focus on particular assessments rather than the entire formative process, and these particular, intentional, and carefully designed assessments are what we are calling *formatives*.

Formatives are intentionally designed to gather evidence based on the scales and are tightly controlled, ensuring as much accuracy in the measurement as possible. Formatives should always be individual and done in class, otherwise we cannot trust the evidence. Though there is controversy in the field around the scoring of formatives (and in general, we believe that the less scoring, the better for learning), we score our formatives and track them in our online gradebook. This allows us to analyze achievement data, form differentiated groups based on this data, provide feedback, and ultimately monitor progress on our chosen learning targets.

As we get closer to the time for the summative, our formatives should look as much like our summative as possible. When preparing for Spamalot, the director doesn't ask students to stand on stage and sing; she provides them with the songs that will be in the final performance. A soccer coach doesn't have students practice in a gym; he has them practice on the field. And before surgical residents perform on live patients, they practice on human cadavers, not mice. Effective instructors try to replicate the conditions of the summative in order to truly prepare their students. That said, it's often necessary to "shrink the field" during practice (to focus on one small part of a skill) so that we can pinpoint a particular part of the learning and determine instructional needs for the whole class and individuals.

THE PRACTICAL PART

DESIGNING PRACTICE

When designing practice activities for students, think about how to maximize comfort early in the learning. This may mean introducing a new skill with familiar or comfortable content. Here are a few examples:

- A middle school social studies teacher wants to introduce students to Google My Maps, an online way to interact with geographical vocabulary, which is her target skill. Eventually, she will ask them to create an itinerary that includes stops at a variety of places to demonstrate understanding of the content language in context. Because this is the first time they have used Google My Maps, however, she decides to take out the pressure of new content in addition to the new skill. Instead, she asks them to create a map that includes highlights from their lives. She gives a few minutes of direct instruction and provides a short list of elements they need to include, but then she has students use the rest of the class to play with Google My Maps. Students learn how to place their pins, add pictures, write descriptions, and color code; they help each other, laugh at pictures they find, share places they've been on vacation, and ask questions; they try, mess up, delete mistakes, try again, and figure it out. None of this is scored, little of this is controlled, and though the content is only vaguely related to the unit, it's relevant to the students and therefore an engaging way to safely play with the new skill. In the next class, the teacher begins to introduce the content vocabulary.

- A fifth-grade teacher cuts out various pictures of scientific models and has her students sort them based on the scale she has introduced. Students create a comprehensive list of what makes an effective model and then work with a partner to create a model that explains why shadows change direction and length. After posting their first drafts around the room, students use the scale and checklist they created to comment on and add suggestions to their peers' work. Pairs then revise their models and give them to the teacher. In just under an hour, students have played with the content, become familiar with the modeling scale, and have developed, assessed, and revised scientific models. None of this is scored, little of this is controlled, and the teacher ends class with a great idea of the next necessary steps.

- A high school Spanish teacher is introducing two new skills to her class: the preterite tense and transition words. She arranges for two other teachers to interrupt her class and after a moment of quiet talk off to the side with lots of pointing, they get in a disagreement about classroom setup and furniture that ends with one of them storming out and threatening to go to the principal. A moment later, the principal returns with the teacher (also prearranged). The principal then asks, "What happened?" The teacher turns to her class and asks them to tell him, in Spanish, what they saw. By now the students have caught on that this is not real, but they are engaged, animated, and excited to recount what happened. They are using vocabulary they are familiar with from a previous unit (classroom vocabulary), but they are having to struggle through tenses and the need for transitions (*then, first, after*) that are new to them. None of this is scored, little other than the setup is controlled, and the content is relevant and engaging. The following class, the teacher introduces the tenses and the transitions that students now have a need to know.

While students are practicing with our skills and content, it's a great time for the teacher to interact with the learning in order to intentionally uncover misunderstandings, holes in the learning, or full-class instructional needs. We should listen to their conversations, ask questions, push students to move beyond their comfort zones, and carefully watch the mistakes they make. This is not usually the time to correct or instruct; ideally, our students forget we are there. Successful practice may be loud, full of movement and laughter, and messy and unpredictable.

Practice does not have to look the same for all students and can be a powerful way to honor individual student preferences. If you know that some students prefer quiet, individual work and others love to work in groups, then provide opportunities for both. (At a conference a few years ago, the presenter mentioned in a side comment that there was no rule that groups had to be the same size. This blew our minds. For 15 years, we had been making same-size groups because . . . well . . . because we would divide the whole by the number of groups we wanted. Turns out, you don't have to do that! You can have a group of one and a few pairs and two groups of six all doing the same task, depending on what you know about your learners. This was liberating.) If some enjoy music playing and others need quiet, allow them to wear headphones. If some need to move and others want to sit on the floor, that's okay. If some need templates and others blank paper, let's give them what they need. The key to practice is that it is low risk, high engagement, and intentionally designed for learning, based on our chosen targets.

DESIGNING FORMATIVES: START WITH YOUR PURPOSE

When designing any assessment, we need to consider what decisions we plan to make based on the evidence we get from the assessment. Rick Stiggins talks about this in terms of our *inferences*. What inferences will we make based on the student work, and how will these inferences drive our instructional choices moving forward? While true for summative assessments as well, this is particularly important when designing formatives, as we already know the learning is not complete and we're looking for evidence to help us plan the next steps for each student. Because the design of our formatives will determine the evidence we get from students and, in turn, drive our instructional choices, we must try to get the most accurate information possible if we want our instruction to be efficient and effective.

One suggestion is to get in the habit of writing the purpose of the assessment for both the students and the teacher on the top of the actual formative. This will become as important for you as it is for the students, holding you accountable to the intent of the assessment and reminding students that their work drives the instructional direction of the class. For example, the purpose of your formative from the student perspective might be *to demonstrate how I intentionally structure my evidence to prove my claim.* This helps you design the task to pinpoint the results you are looking for and helps students stay focused on the target. The purpose of the assessment from the teacher perspective may be *the results of this formative will help determine what instruction and practice we still need before next week's summative.* Being explicit about purpose can help hold you accountable for responding to the results and reminds students that their work directly drives what happens next in class.

SHRINK THE FIELD

Once you have determined the purpose of the assessment for the students and how you plan to use the results, it's time to shrink the assessment field. We do not want to cloud our inferences with too many interwoven skills or make false inferences based on irrelevant skills or content. So, start with a single scale and consider how to most efficiently find out where students are in relation to the target.

In the following example, we were gearing up for an essay about the relationship between the ideas of Locke and Hobbes and the novel *Lord of the Flies.* We had been working on how to choose and use evidence most effectively to prove a claim, and it was time to see if they could independently select evidence and justify its use. Because evidence was our focus for this formative, we needed to remove as much distraction as we could, so we chose to provide claims rather than have them make their own. Because we were specifically interested in their awareness of the reason for their choices around evidence, we created a chart that would force them to justify rather than analyze (see Figure 6.1). Had we asked for this in paragraph form, we may have confused students who are used to analyzing evidence, which is not what we were looking for.

FIGURE 6.1   Formative Assessment Example

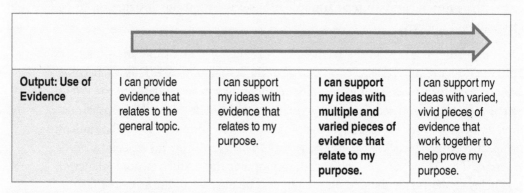

Justifying Evidence

Purpose: to demonstrate how I intentionally structure my evidence to prove my claim

Use of the results: The results of this formative will determine what instruction and practice we still need before next week's summative. We will have some differentiated group work on Monday, based on needs.

Output: Use of Evidence	I can provide evidence that relates to the general topic.	I can support my ideas with evidence that relates to my purpose.	**I can support my ideas with multiple and varied pieces of evidence that relate to my purpose.**	I can support my ideas with varied, vivid pieces of evidence that work together to help prove my purpose.

Task: Choose one of the following thesis statements and complete the chart, finding evidence to support the thesis and then justifying it:

- Ralph and Jack are more alike than they are different.
- The boys' attitudes toward the beast represent their differing beliefs about human nature.
- As civilization starts to fall apart, Ralph begins to rely more on his relationship with Piggy.
- Despite trying to remain good, Ralph has the same capacity for evil as the other boys.

Chosen Thesis:	
Evidence: Include your set up, your quote, and the citation.	**Justification:** Why you chose this piece of evidence and why you are using it in the order you have chosen.

By shrinking the field, we are much more likely to get an accurate picture of each student's current ability with this skill, and thus, we are much more likely to design appropriate, targeted instruction that will help each student improve.

PROVIDE FEEDBACK

Feedback is vital to learning. We cannot improve without feedback. But feedback does not have to mean hours and hours spent making comments on work. In fact, most research and experience show that this is almost always an inefficient and ineffective way to provide feedback. If you subscribe to the belief that the one doing is the one learning, then the thousands of hours I spent making comments on student essays means a ton of learning was done—by me. Editing work, making corrections for students, or even pointing out errors will lead to little student growth. We need to ensure that the time we spend providing feedback leads to timely, specific, and effective student action.

Feedback should be timely. Think of learning how to juggle. You take three balls and throw them all into the air. You catch one, but the others fall. Immediate feedback—it didn't work. You try again, this time holding onto one and throwing the other two in the air. You fail again. Immediate feedback. How did you know you failed? Because you know what it looks like when someone succeeds at juggling. You can see the target and you compare yourself to that target right now. You don't have to wait a week to find out how you did. Video games are successful for this very reason. They provide clear, immediate feedback; players know the goal (get to Level 2) and they can see how to get there.

How do we bring that immediacy into the classroom? By changing our definition of *feedback*. We do not need to collect everything and score everything and comment on everything. Instead, we need to design practice opportunities and a class structure that allow us to see the learning and provide feedback (a quick comment, a redirection, small group instruction, targeted practice) as soon as possible. That means that class should be the time when students are doing and we are watching them do. Does this mean "flipped" classes, where we deliver content outside of class? No. It means rethinking how we use our time so that students access our content by being more than receptacles to our delivery. For example, rather than giving a lecture or PowerPoint about the Boxer Rebellion or photosynthesis, provide students with a thesis statement and three resources and have them find the evidence themselves. They do the learning and you watch, redirect, correct misconceptions, and provide immediate feedback. At the end of class, you can collect their notes, sort them into piles, and really target your instruction the next day based on student need. And you don't need to score any of that.

When you do give a formative assessment, one that you have intentionally designed to gather individual evidence of targeted achievement, you can provide feedback using well-written scales. When students are practiced at using the language of the scale to assess their own work, they can use them to guide their next steps. Consider handing back formatives with the next-step box highlighted instead of the current achievement. This trains students to see each formative as a check-in on the way to the next destination. Removing numbers or labels from the levels also helps emphasize this mindset. We quickly found that giving feedback on a 1–4 scale using numbers was little better than our old grading. Students ignored the language in the scale that we worked so hard to get right and only saw the number. Simply replacing those numbers with an arrow forced students to look at the language and ask questions about the skill, not the number. There was no more "How do I get to the 4?" Instead, it became "How do I vary my evidence more in order to prove my claim?"

DEVELOP TASK SHEETS

Task sheets are an important organizational and feedback tool in a proficiency-based classroom and can be used for practice, formative, or summative tasks. They are created by the teacher but are vital for students and support staff as well.

Here's what most task sheets include (but you can make your own, of course!).

- **Lesson Purpose**: At the top of the task sheet, it's important to clearly state the lesson goal or purpose. This is different than the activity, and more specific than the target. Consider why students are doing this activity and how it will move them forward on the scale. The purpose often links the content being studied with the skill that is being practiced and can remind students how the evidence from the task will be used to plan instruction.

- **Scale(s)**: Cut and paste the applicable scale(s) at the top of the sheet. This way students know the skill(s) they should be focused on while completing the task.

- **Task**: This is where you explain what the task is; be as specific as necessary for your learners. At times, you may need to differentiate the task based on data from earlier formative assessments.

In addition, some teachers include the following:

- **An Executive Functioning Element:** If you want to help students work on time management, consider adding suggested times with a space for them to write in actual times. You can also have a place for pre-thinking, organization, or other planning that needs to take place prior to the task.

- **A Self-Assessment Direction**: When students finish the task, some teachers ask them to assess their work using the scale(s) on the task sheet and provide an explanation of their assessment.

- **A Space for Reflection or Questions:** Some teachers ask students to write down questions they still have after the task or to reflect on the experience.

EXAMPLE

Figure 6.2 gives an example of a task sheet.

FIGURE 6.2   Task Sheet Example

Geopolitics Task Sheet: Mining Information for Context, Understanding, and Application

"Our students do not know how to write because they do not know how to think." —Tony Wagner

Purpose: We will spend the next few classes practicing how to explore and understand information at deep levels. We will begin the process on paper in groups of four, progress to groups of two, and end by transitioning to individual annotations.

Target Practiced:

Champlain Valley Union (CVU) Graduation Standard	Getting Started	Making Progress	**Proficient**	Transfer
2.b. Analyze, evaluate, and synthesize information from multiple sources to build on knowledge.	I am reading complex texts with insufficient knowledge and understanding.	I can mine complex texts for various layers of meaning, showing comprehension on language and content.	**I can mine complex texts for multiple layers of meaning, showing comprehension of language and content. I can analyze the cause and effect of geopolitical relationships.**	I can mine complex texts for multiple layers of meaning, showing comprehension of language and content. I can analyze the cause and effect of multiple geopolitical relationships and their effect on the international community.

Task: Individually scan the 2014 article, *Geopolitics and the New World Order* by Robert D. Kaplan (Senior Fellow at the Center for a New American Security in Washington, DC). In your group, discuss one or two main points *you think* the article makes.

Step 1: Together, take the handout of the enlarged first paragraph of the article and glue it down in the middle of the white sheet of paper provided.

Step 2: Begin mining the paragraph for information. Use arrows, Venn diagrams, circles, boxes, highlighters— anything to identify, analyze, and draw meaning from the content. Ask questions: What do I need to know to understand what the author is saying? What vocabulary should I define? What modern and historical factors must I research? How does this paragraph connect to the title of the article? Ask questions, make inferences and hypotheses, and most of all: *THINK!*

Step 3: When you are done, call me over to review your work and provide feedback.

Here's how task sheets are helpful:

- **For Teachers:** This is a great way to stay organized, intentional, and focused on the targets. Once you have a basic template created, these are quick and easy to create and share with or print for students, to link to class websites, or to share with special educators or paraprofessionals. Task sheets are also a great way to provide feedback on the task, as the scale is right there (many teachers collect work with the task sheet stapled to the top and then use it to provide the feedback directly). Task sheets also allow for easy differentiation, as teachers can create multiple sheets based on need.

- **For Students:** Students benefit from the clarity and the targeted focus of the task. They say they love knowing what they are doing and why and that they can refer to the task sheet when they get lost. Task sheets allow them to work at their own pace, stay on task, and easily make up work when absent.

- **For Support Staff or Special Educators**: Teachers can work with special educators to modify or scaffold tasks easily when the purpose and scale are provided.

USE EXIT CARDS

Let's say I have a class activity that involves students working in groups to gather research based on a provided thesis. The target that they are focusing on is about using the best evidence to support a thesis. Here's how I might formatively assess their work: About 10 minutes before the end of class, I will hand out an index card. I will ask students to write the one piece of evidence that they think is the best on one side and a piece of evidence they think is not very good on the other; then I will ask them to explain why they chose each based on the thesis. That's it. It's important that this is done individually—it's okay (even beneficial) to have students work in groups often, but our assessment of their knowledge, understanding, or skill needs to be individual.

Now that I have the index cards, it will take me 5–10 minutes to go through them and put them in three piles: those who nailed it, those who are close, and those who aren't there yet. This is the start of my planning for the next class.

BE INTENTIONAL ABOUT HOMEWORK

Nothing gets teachers, parents, and students fired up more than homework. One of the reasons for this is the contradictory research findings that seem to suggest that homework both supports and prevents learning, both encourages and discourages effective habits, and is both emotionally healthy and emotionally destructive. As intelligent people who all want the best for our kids, what are we to believe?

We suggest you base your homework practices and policies on the following:

- research about the brain and learning
- research about child and adolescent development
- good old-fashioned common sense

The research about the first two can be found fairly easily (we suggest James Zull's *The Art of Changing the Brain* [2002], Eric Jensen's *Teaching with the Brain in Mind* [2008], David Sousa's *How the Brain Learns* [2017], and Thomas Armstrong's *The Power of the Adolescent Brain* [2016]). In a nutshell, we know that learners need time to consolidate learning, that learning needs to be within the zone of proximal development, that engagement is a significant driver of learning (particularly during adolescence), and that the brain wants a target. This knowledge alone has to change our beliefs and practices around homework.

Common sense should also drive our decisions about homework. Common sense tells us that at certain levels or ages, homework could very well have a positive impact on learning. However, we also know that for learning to be positively affected by homework, it needs to be high-quality homework. All homework is not created equal. And let's be honest—we all think *our* work isn't busy work. But if our homework isn't created or assigned based on what we know about learning, if we cannot ensure that it is done independently, and if it isn't directly used to inform instruction, then there's a pretty good chance it is, in fact, busy work.

Here are a few common-sense considerations that may help you define your beliefs about homework in a standards-based class:

- **Rigor:** More is not always better. The classes that give the most homework are not the most rigorous. This is a huge misunderstanding, one it's time we stop perpetuating. More does not equal harder; difficulty is not the same thing as complexity. If I want to make reading more difficult for a student, I can double the amount, make the font twice as small, or demand that he or she read it upside down. If I want to make reading more complex, I can find a text at a higher reading level or I can ask that my student think about the reading in a more complex way. Fifty math problems are not more rigorous than five math problems. A ten-page essay is not more rigorous than a two-page essay.

- **Time:** For years, we have heard that students should have 10 minutes of homework per grade. So, a first grader should have 10 minutes, a seventh grader 70 minutes, and a twelfth grader 120 minutes. While the simplicity of this rule is seductive, does it make sense? We know that learning is not time dependent. For some students, a task that we intend to take 30 minutes will actually take three times that. For others, less time. So, if we are going to play by the 10-minute rule, we need to be assigning tasks that are not time-dependent. In other words, we need to tell students that finishing a task is not the goal (and then we need to stand by that, not punishing or rewarding students based on what they have finished—not taking away recess or free time because a task we assigned for homework is incomplete). For example, asking students to read for 25 minutes is okay; asking them to read four chapters may not be. Also, this rule does not mean 10 minutes per class per grade. It's total. That means if a student in ninth grade has eight classes a day, then each teacher should be expecting just over 10 minutes for their individual class; in a four-block day, that means about 20 minutes of work per class.

- **Life:** We know students are busy outside of the traditional school day. Kids have family responsibilities, jobs, chores, sports, music, clubs, and after-school programs. All of these things enrich our students' lives and provide avenues for them to learn incredibly valuable life skills; we want to encourage these activities, not have students opt out because they're too busy. But a typical sixth-grade child may attend school from 7:30 a.m. to 3:00 p.m., go to an after-school activity until 5:00 p.m., get home and settled by 5:30 p.m., then be in bed by 8:00 p.m. That leaves a possible two and a half hours of awake time *in the entire day* that is not school controlled. Add dinner, chores, and 60 minutes of homework and those hours are gone. As teachers, we often lament the lack of creativity and imagination in our students, and yet we allow so little time for them to be imaginative outside of our classrooms. Kids need time to be kids, even big kids. They need time to play and imagine and be bored. They need time to socialize and wander and explore. They need time to dive into learning they choose. And they also need time to sleep.

- **Habits:** Despite pockets of research that say homework teaches students to have effective habits, common sense says this is probably not true. Homework more often rewards or punishes existing habits and sometimes speaks more to the habits of the parents than of the students. If our goal is to help students learn time management and organizational skills, there are many ways to do that that are more effective, measurable, and equitable than homework. In addition, what we know about child and adolescent learning tells us that humans do not fully develop their executive functioning skills until their early 20s, so asking students to be good at these skills at age eight or 12 or even 17 may be developmentally inappropriate.

- **Preparation for the Real World:** Many teachers and parents say homework is necessary because it prepares students for what comes next. In middle school, we say we need to assign homework to prepare students for high school, and in high school, we say we need even more to prepare them for college. The best way to prepare students for the rigorous work and complex thinking they will encounter in the future is to teach them how to ask questions, how to think critically, and how to learn. We don't need tons of homework to do this. In fact, we can do this much more effectively within our classrooms.

You can probably find research to back your opinion about homework, regardless of your beliefs (unless you teach K–4, in which case, there is growing consensus that homework is not beneficial), and while all this contradictory information could be viewed as frustrating, why not view it as liberating? Let's use what we know as professionals—not what was done to us or what we've always done—combined with our common sense to develop homework policies or belief systems that we (and our families) feel good about. We need to make sure our choices support what we know about learning, that they are true to standards-based and differentiated principles, and that they respect our students as busy young people.

Challenges

Guilt: Good formative assessment practice can lead to a lot of guilt. When we determine success based on the quality of student learning rather than the quality of our teaching, we will quickly realize that we're going to fall short. Nothing points this out like a well-designed formative. When teachers get that first set of student work—or the fifth—and realize that students are all over the place, they realize they have to do something about it. And that's inconvenient. It means they may need to slow down or speed up, return to something they already taught or skip something coming up, or take extra time to plan and run differentiated lessons. And they don't have time for that. In the past, we could push on, rationalizing the pacing or quality of our instruction by focusing on the students that were getting it and hoping it would snap together for the others before the test. But when formative assessments truly drive what we do next, we cannot rationalize away the evidence of learning. Because most teachers want to do the right thing, this can be paralyzing. One of the best pieces of advice we've heard is from Rick Wormeli. At a conference last year, he told a room full of eager but overwhelmed teachers that they had to do the right thing 51% of the time and then they should sleep well at night. We have to give ourselves permission to do the best we can and forgive ourselves when 51% is all we can do.

They Won't Do It If I Don't Grade It: The trouble with this challenge is that it can be true at first, particularly if you are the only teacher that is standards based. We need to remember that for many students, we are changing the rules of a game they have been experts at for the majority of their lives. We are asking them to think about scoring and grading as communication, not compensation. This is a tough paradigm shift. This challenge can also be true if teachers change their grading but not their instruction and assessment. If assignments are not targeted, differentiated, and seem to have no connection to their success as learners, then chances are they will not be seen as a priority. But when your class is truly standards based in teaching, learning, and grading, this problem disappears. Students will do work that is meaningful, clear, and leads to success. There is a significant difference between *not grading* and *optional*. Teachers still need to set the expectation that the work is a mandatory part of the learning cycle; and when it isn't finished or accurate, students will need to do it (even if that means we rearrange our class time to get it done). Additionally, because we are not grading formative work does not mean we aren't providing feedback—if we assign it, we should be using it to ensure learning and catch misunderstandings, not only to check for compliance.

The Guilt-Free Box

Overwhelmed by the thought of being so intentional all the time? Worried about how much more time effective feedback takes? Can't imagine differentiating homework?

Consider these starting points:

- Don't change your homework policy, but start paying attention to it. Ask students for feedback about the effectiveness of what you are assigning. Ask them how long it takes them. See if you can connect it to your learning targets each time you assign it.

- Start simple with task sheets. Create one at the beginning of the unit and then cut and paste elements in as you go, changing out the scales. You can cut parts out if they are overwhelming and only include the basics.

Design Effective Instruction

We all laughed when we saw Ben Stein's portrayal of a teacher in *Ferris Bueller's Day Off*:

> In 1930, the Republican controlled House of Representatives, in an effort to alleviate the effects of the . . . Anyone? Anyone? . . . Great Depression . . . passed the . . . Anyone? Anyone? Tariff Bill, the Hawley Smoot Tariff Act. . . . (Hughes, 1986)

The unfortunate reason for our laughter was that the scene likely rang all too true for us, not only as students, but as teachers. It is not difficult to quickly flash back to classes such as this where we were the passive receptacles, and I can think of many times when I was also the teacher in that scene.

Today, many still consider instruction to mean a teacher lecturing and a student dutifully taking notes or at least not causing any trouble. In essence, instruction has really been a teacher telling the class what they know about a subject and hoping that the majority of students memorize that knowledge for a test. We now know that the one doing is the one learning, and as long as it's the teacher talking, it's the teacher learning. Long lectures or PowerPoints on the causes of World War I, photosynthesis, or *Of Mice and Men* are no longer appropriate if our goal is deep, transferable learning for students. We need to find ways to switch the *doing* to the students during all phases of learning.

[**GLOSSARY OF KEY TERMS**]

Input, Critical Thinking, Output: Based on work we have done at our school, we have come to think about the process of learning in these three stages. First, learners must *input* content into their brains, which they can do in multiple ways. Next, learners must

(Continued)

(Continued)

make sense of this content, analyzing, synthesizing, evaluating, and ultimately creating new thoughts (in other words, *critical thinking*). Finally, learners must communicate their thoughts (through writing, speaking, creating) and this is their *output*. For real learning to happen, output must be greater than input, which only happens when there is critical thinking going on.

Differentiation by Readiness: Though there are multiple types of differentiation (readiness, learning profile, interest), we will focus specifically on differentiation by readiness in this section. Differentiating by readiness means that we must shift instruction or practice based on evidence from intentionally designed assessments in order to meet the needs of students at multiple levels on our scales. Readiness differentiation is not the same as tracking, and we will discuss this difference in Chapter 8.

FURTHER EXPLORATION

Doug Fisher and Nancy Frey: In Fisher and Frey's book, *Better Learning Through Structured Teaching* (2014), they discuss the gradual release of responsibility. We will briefly discuss the concept behind this important strategy (I do it. We do it. You do it together. You do it alone.); however, this book will dive into details that will further help you implement this in class. Fisher and Frey are also amazing presenters who have taught together for years. They have many practical strategies for instruction, assessment, and feedback, all tested in their own classroom. We still use many of their suggestions, including foldables (shout out to Fairbanks Core!), and their work belongs in every professional library.

James E. Zull: Zull's book *The Art of Changing the Brain* (2002) is one of our all-time favorites. His in-depth look into the relationship between neuroscience and teaching has had an enormous impact on teachers everywhere. When you read the science behind learning, the changes in education we discuss seem not only exciting but absolutely necessary. This is a great read cover to cover, but there are multiple chapters we have used in professional development over and over to help convince skeptical teachers that our practices need to change. Having Zull's words at your fingertips could be exactly what you need to persuade the seemingly unpersuadable.

Carol Ann Tomlinson: I know we included Carol Ann Tomlinson in Section I, but we must include her here as well since she wrote the book, literally, on differentiation—dozens of them, actually. If you get a chance to go to a conference with her, do so. But if you can't get to a conference, we suggest starting with *The Differentiated Classroom* (2016), *Differentiation in Practice* (2003), or *Integrating Differentiated Instruction Understanding by Design* (coauthored by Jay McTighe, 2006).

Rick Wormeli: Rick Wormeli's book, *Differentiation* (2007), was the first book on this topic that we read, and it's still a great primer on the *why, what,* and *how* of good responsive teaching. But if you can only get one of his books, we strongly suggest the latest edition of *Fair Isn't Always Equal* (2018), which is a must read for so many reasons. Wormeli's words and wisdom about differentiation will always be foundational for our profession. And he is super fun to see in person—a performer and an inspiration!

David Sousa: Like James Zull, Sousa's focus in *How the Brain Learns* (2017) is not specifically on instruction and is more about the underlying principles of learning that support our instructional choices. His understanding of neuroscience and the workings of the brain at all levels can guide teachers to evaluate their current practices and make shifts that support what we know about learning. We are strong believers that understanding the brain and learning is the key to understanding the importance of the changes standards-based learning requires in our classrooms.

Judy Willis: Both a neurologist and a classroom teacher, Willis combines her scientific expertise with her practical experience in the book, *Research-Based Strategies to Ignite Student Learning* (2006). This is a small book in size but is large in ideas, and we really appreciate her logical approach to the brain-based suggestions she makes about learning and teaching. It's another great book to have in your library for teachers who want to see "the research."

CHAPTER 7

Designing Instruction

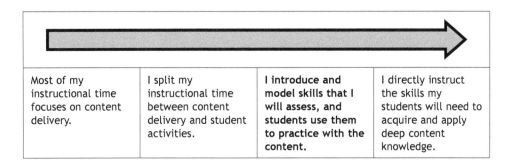

| Most of my instructional time focuses on content delivery. | I split my instructional time between content delivery and student activities. | **I introduce and model skills that I will assess, and students use them to practice with the content.** | I directly instruct the skills my students will need to acquire and apply deep content knowledge. |

COMMENTARY AND CONTEXT

Years ago, we worked with about a dozen teachers from all discipline areas to develop a model for learning at our school that we hoped would drive instructional changes in our classrooms. We started by asking what we wanted from our students at the end of their time with us, whether that was a semester, a year, or four years. Not surprisingly, the answers were not that they know when the New Deal was, can name the parts of the cell, or can list the symbols in *Lord of the Flies*. While we all agreed that the content was important, our hopes for our students were much grander. We wanted students who could use knowledge to analyze texts, evaluate bias, adapt communication based on audience, graphically represent ideas, model phenomena, and think critically about issues. We wanted students who could make sense of difficult material, synthesize large amounts of understanding, and express their ideas with clarity and eloquence. We wanted students who could ask the questions our communities need to hear and solve the problems of our world. In short, we wanted students who could thrive outside of the walls of our school.

FIGURE 7.1 The Big Blue Head

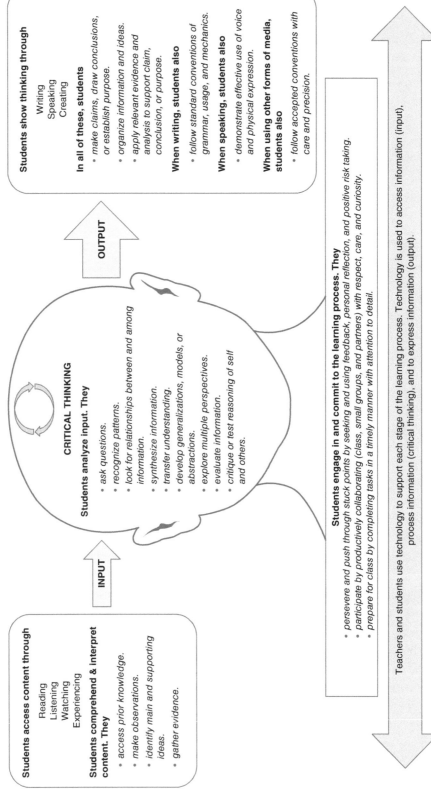

LEARNING at CVU: A common framework to guide instruction and assessment (DRAFT)

Students access content through

Reading
Listening
Watching
Experiencing

Students comprehend & interpret content. They

• access prior knowledge.
• make observations.
• identify main and supporting ideas.
• gather evidence.

CRITICAL THINKING

Students analyze input. They

• ask questions.
• recognize patterns.
• look for relationships between and among information.
• synthesize information.
• transfer understanding.
• develop generalizations, models, or abstractions.
• explore multiple perspectives.
• evaluate information.
• critique or test reasoning of self and others.

INPUT

OUTPUT

Students show thinking through

Writing
Speaking
Creating

In all of these, students

• make claims, draw conclusions, or establish purpose.
• organize information and ideas.
• apply relevant evidence and analysis to support claim, conclusion, or purpose.

When writing, students also

• follow standard conventions of grammar, usage, and mechanics.

When speaking, students also

• demonstrate effective use of voice and physical expression.

When using other forms of media, students also

• follow accepted conventions with care and precision.

Students engage in and commit to the learning process. They

• persevere and push through stuck points by seeking and using feedback, personal reflection, and positive risk taking.
• participate by productively collaborating (class, small groups, and partners) with respect, care, and curiosity.
• prepare for class by completing tasks in a timely manner with attention to detail.

Teachers and students use technology to support each stage of the learning process. Technology is used to access information (input), process information (critical thinking), and to express information (output).

Once we came up with our hopes for our students, we organized them, categorized them, revised them, and created a rough visual to represent the relationship between and among these learning goals. One of the teachers suggested we organize them around a head, another suggested we copy the draft on blue paper, and voila! The Big Blue Head was born (see Figure 7.1).

Over the next three years, the Big Blue Head went through a variety of committees, was used with students throughout the school, and was revised over and over. The result is a model that has helped inform the way we think about both teaching and learning, and that ultimately drove the creation of our school's graduation standards. Though we moved away from the model in our formal standards documents, you can still find it hanging in many classrooms, driving our thinking about learning.

There are three main parts to the Big Blue Head, and understanding each part allowed us to be more intentional in our instructional design. Knowing where in the learning process our skills or even our activities fell helped us remove distractions from our main purpose. While all three are constantly overlapping—and it's impossible in reality to separate them from each other—the simplicity of the model helped us ensure that we were instructing what we intended to instruct.

INPUT

Learning requires input. When we ask students how they take in content during school, they most often reply, "Reading and listening." In fact, many will say they spend most of their time in school doing these tasks. But there are other ways to get content into our heads as well, and limiting our learning targets to this pair of common skills discounts all of the ways we as learners take in what we want to (or have to) learn. By switching our language to *input* (rather than *reading*), we can recognize that the vehicle for the input is often of secondary importance to the effectiveness; if the goal is to get stuff in our heads so we can think about it, then it doesn't always matter whether we do this through reading, listening, watching, experiencing, or a combination of them all.

Thinking of input as the first step in learning can change our instruction in significant ways. Students need something relevant, rich, and rigorous to think about: our content. But if we are truly going to prepare them for life outside of school, then we need to teach them how to access and understand content on their own, not package it in a lecture or a PowerPoint and present it to them. This is the first step in changing instruction, switching from input *delivery* (where the teacher decides the content, organizes it, and delivers it to the student through lecture, PowerPoint, or readings) to input *discovery* (where the teacher designs essential questions or claims, and students find, understand, and organize the content). The problem? The first is so much easier and so much more predictable.

CRITICAL THINKING

In our first 15 years of teaching, we spent the overwhelming majority of classroom time focusing on input and output not only in our instruction but in our assessment as well. We assumed the thinking. We would lecture, assign reading, or deliver beautifully designed PowerPoints, and then either prepare a test or assign a project or an essay or some other form of output. And then we assessed the output. Sure, we might have some activities that demanded critical thinking or we might have told students to analyze something, but we rarely, if ever, spent time instructing and intentionally practicing critical thinking skills.

While students critically think throughout the learning process, until we can isolate these thinking skills, we will not be able to instruct them successfully. The Big Blue Head model takes a stab at defining *thinking*, breaking it down into a set of distinct, teachable skills. Once we've defined these skills, we can write learning targets and scales to help us and our students understand what they mean, what they look like, and how to improve. So often in middle and high school, students' thinking skills develop faster than their abilities to express that thinking; because we so often measure thinking through output, we can misdiagnose student achievement and make assumptions based on these diagnoses. If we want to help challenge all students and honor the thinking that our students are capable of, we need to learn how to instruct and assess critical thinking.

Critical thinking should be the messiest part of the learning and, ideally, the part that takes the longest. We have to give students time to play with the input and time to practice the skills involved in critical thinking if we want to see their output improve.

OUTPUT

Traditionally, student success was based almost entirely on output skills. We measured learning through writing, speaking, or some other form of expression. Arguably, there is no other way to measure learning, as students need to express it in order for us to measure it. Knowing this should lead us to much more intentional instruction of the expressive skills students need in order to share their knowledge, understanding, and achievement.

The biggest change in instruction of output skills in a standards-based class is the intentionality (seems to be a theme of standards-based learning [SBL], doesn't it?). If we know we will be asking students to share their thinking through writing, for instance, we must ensure that the writing does not hinder the ability of students to share that thinking. If we are assigning a poster, then we need to ensure that we instruct the skills involved in poster making. Assuming that students have the output skills necessary to demonstrate their understanding of our content could lead to inaccurate assessment of that understanding.

THE PRACTICAL PART

There are so many great instructional strategies out there, and every teacher has their favorites. Often, success with certain strategies depends upon teacher comfort, preference, and personality, but there are a few shifts in instruction that can be adapted to most personalities and that will significantly increase learning in each of the three phases of learning: input, critical thinking, and output. We are going to focus on three instructional shifts with specific strategies that have led to success for teachers across disciplines and grade levels in our district.

SHIFT FROM TEACHER TO STUDENT

Strategy: Gradual Release of Responsibility

You may already be familiar with this incredible way of thinking about instruction, first developed by Pearson and Gallagher for reading instruction in the 1980s and then brought more widely to our profession by Doug Fisher and Nancy Frey a few decades later. The underlying purpose of the model is to shift responsibility from the teacher to the student through a four-step instructional process: focused instruction (I do it), guided instruction (We do it), collaborative learning (You do it together), and independent learning (You do it alone).

The gradual release model beautifully meshes with SBL. One of the most valuable ways to instruct a skill is to help students feel the difference between and among the levels on the scale, and by following the four steps, teachers can help students experience success early in the learning. Here's how it might play out in a standards-based class:

Learning Target: Graphic Representation

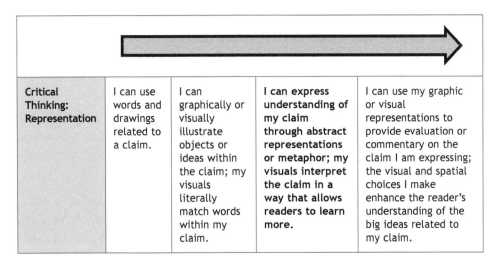

Critical Thinking: Representation	I can use words and drawings related to a claim.	I can graphically or visually illustrate objects or ideas within the claim; my visuals literally match words within my claim.	I can express understanding of my claim through abstract representations or metaphor; my visuals interpret the claim in a way that allows readers to learn more.	I can use my graphic or visual representations to provide evaluation or commentary on the claim I am expressing; the visual and spatial choices I make enhance the reader's understanding of the big ideas related to my claim.

Step 1: Focused Instruction. The teacher begins by introducing the highest level of the scale through a relevant, engaging model. The goal in this step is to show students what it looks like to be successful in this skill and to introduce the language of the scale. Using content that the students are familiar with or that is highly engaging and relevant to them, the teacher presents and talks about the model.

For example, our students had just completed a unit where they wrote about the role of morality in historical progress, so here, we used that content to model the graphic representation target. We started with a claim, which was also one of the understandings from our K-U-D ([know, understand, do], *Innovation leads to both progress and destruction*), and then created a graphic (see Figure 7.2).

FIGURE 7.2   Graphic Representation of *Innovation leads to both progress and destruction*.

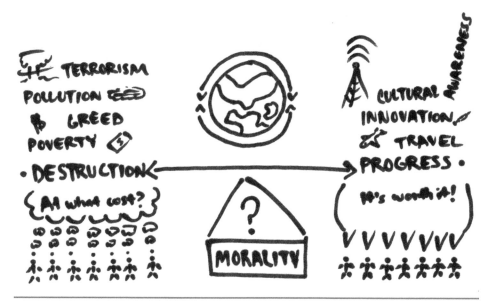

Image adapted from original by Kirsten Nestor.

Once students saw the graphic and had a few minutes to look at it, we discussed the following, which are all words/concepts directly from the scale:

- **Understanding:** We talked about how captions and labels help enhance understanding and suggested other captions we could have used that would have changed the understanding. We reviewed the difference between *labels* and *captions* and why you might use each.

- **Big Idea(s):** We talked about the big ideas we had chosen to include and referenced a previous target about big ideas. We discussed the relationship between those big ideas and how the graphic showed that relationship. We talked about why we chose to use balance as our central metaphor.

- **Commentary or Evaluation:** We talked about the difference between objective representation and subjective commentary; we reviewed what *evaluation* meant, referencing a past learning target. We discussed what the graphic showed about truth, humanity, morality, and the complexity of progress. We talked about the theme that could transcend the specific content.

After showing our model and using the language of the scale to talk about the choices we made, students asked clarifying questions and suggested edits. Then we came up with a list of hints and suggestions for the graphic representation skill and we posted these at the front of the room.

Step 2: Guided Instruction. Now that students had seen a model, it was time to work together as a class. We handed out copies of the scale that included space beneath each level to work (we used 11×17 paper to ensure that there was enough room). In order to save some time, we included the Level 4 graphic we had modeled beneath the Level 4 descriptor, and then we worked together to develop Levels 1, 2, and 3. Our goal was to have them feel the differences and experience the progression. We asked one student to do this on the board while the rest of the class made suggestions. When we finished, each student had a document with examples at each level of the scale that they could use when working independently (see Figure 7.3).

FIGURE 7.3   Models Placed on a Scale

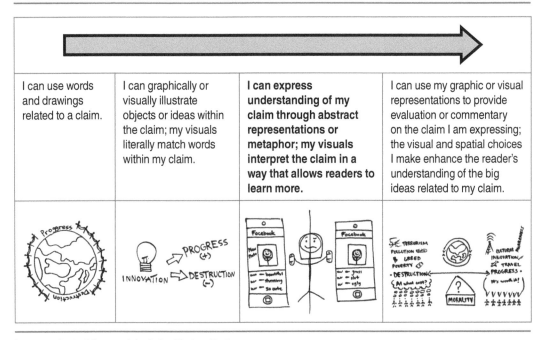

Images adapted from originals by Kirsten Nestor.

Step 3: Collaborative Learning. There are two main purposes for this step of the model. First, the students are able to play with the new skill in a safe and social way. The adolescent brain craves social interactions, and when students are allowed to talk and think together, they are often more likely to retain what they learned. Second, the teacher is able to catch early misunderstandings and identify full-class instructional needs. For our activity, we paired students and gave them a new claim and a blank scale with space for work (printed on the back of the original 11×17). Together, they worked through the progression as we walked around and listened for misconceptions, guided their choices, and pushed thinking. It became clear to us during this phase that the majority of students were still really struggling with the difference between captions and labels, so we knew we needed to start the next class with a mini-lesson and some clarification. This phase of the model also allowed us to gather more student examples to use as we continued to work on the skill.

Step 4: Independent Learning. Once students have had a chance to play with the skill and we have corrected major misunderstandings, it's time for students to attempt the skill on their own. If we want to be able to determine where each student is in relation to the target, we need to have an individual formative assessment. We provided a new claim and asked students for all four levels on this formative—as we had in the practice—in order to see where they were getting stuck, which allowed us to differentiate in subsequent classes.

The gradual release of responsibility model of instruction has been a clear and effective way to introduce complex skills to our students and provide scaffolding early in the learning. Any phase of this model can be sped up or slowed down, and we have even found ourselves merging steps occasionally based on need, time restraints, or purpose.

SHIFT FROM ASSUMING TO ENSURING

Rather than assuming that our students are thinking critically about our content when we tell them to, we need to ensure that they are doing so, which means treating critical thinking skills like any other skills and defining them clearly, articulating the skill progression, and providing lots of time to instruct and practice. While there are many ways to teach what it means to analyze, synthesize, compare, contrast, and evaluate, we have found one way that allows us to flexibly instruct students based on our purpose. This strategy works at any level and in any discipline and can easily be adapted to fit most instructional needs and content. Even though we use it for critical thinking mostly, it's also a great way to guide input and plan for output.

Strategy: Tiles

Tiles play on the best aspects of mind mapping but add physical manipulation and the ability to take risks with thinking. At their most basic, tiles are slips of paper (we prefer cardstock) with words or phrases on them. Usually the words and phrases are determined by the teacher, but there are times when students choose or determine their own. We are going to show one way to use tiles to instruct critical thinking skills, but as you will see, the strategy is flexible enough to adapt to about any purpose or content area.

Evaluating Relationships in an English Class

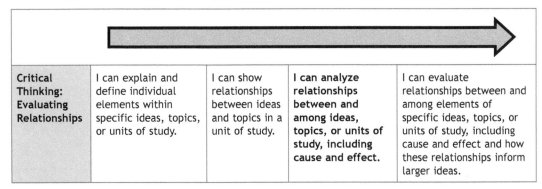

Critical Thinking: Evaluating Relationships	I can explain and define individual elements within specific ideas, topics, or units of study.	I can show relationships between ideas and topics in a unit of study.	I can analyze relationships between and among ideas, topics, or units of study, including cause and effect.	I can evaluate relationships between and among elements of specific ideas, topics, or units of study, including cause and effect and how these relationships inform larger ideas.

An English teacher's class had read *In the Heart of the Sea* by Nathaniel Philbrick, and she used tiles to help the students develop complex claims. Students were given tiles that were color coded: blue for characters and green for big ideas. In addition, they were given sticky notes to use for quotes and blank tiles so that they could add ideas that matched their thinking. The class had been working on the evaluating relationships learning target, and their task was to evaluate the relationships between and among the characters and main ideas in the book in order to develop complex claims that would eventually drive their essays.

The students spent the next two class periods arranging tiles, thinking, testing their ideas, finding evidence, rearranging tiles based on their evidence, drafting working thesis statements, rearranging tiles again based on the thesis, revising the thesis based on their evidence, and ultimately committing to both a thesis and a critical thinking map. Once committed, students glued their tiles to the paper and spent the next class period explaining their thinking through writing, symbols, and placement of tiles (see Figure 7.4 on the next page).

What's different about using tiles instead of traditional mind mapping is that they encourage students to change their minds. They can try out different relationships and connections without committing to them. When mapping with pen and paper or on a computer screen, the placement of concepts and words is fixed. Sure, you can erase or delete or cut and paste, but there's a difference. Students are not afraid to try out their thoughts—which is what they should be doing. We want to teach them to think deeply and critically about what we read and study, and so they must be able to practice that thinking in a safe way.

FIGURE 7.4   Example of the Tiles Strategy

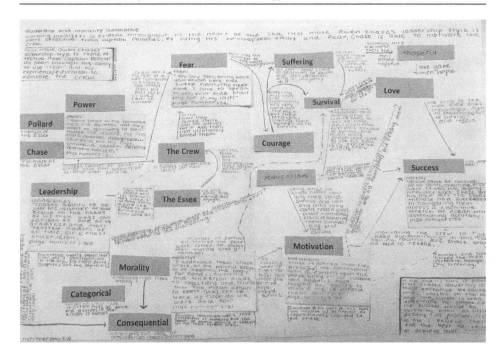

In addition, there is a physical component in play here that is missing with traditional mapping; students are physically moving the parts around. They quickly see the difference between placing two tiles touching each other and placing them a foot away from each other. Some start to get creative with their placement, adding 3D components or placing some tiles upside down to show contradictions. From a teaching perspective, what we can tell about our students' understanding from a tile activity far surpasses what we can tell from writing, discussion, or other forms of assessment.

There are many other ways to use tiles. Teachers turn them into games, select tiles for different students in order to differentiate, increase rigor by adding more complex concept tiles, use them as a way to understand relationships among vocabulary words, or use them to encourage discussion.

One suggestion we have: Do not get cute and think that different-shaped tiles would be a good idea—they take forever to cut out.

SHIFT FROM SECRECY TO TRANSPARENCY

One of the most important instructional shifts we can make is also one of the simplest in theory: Show students what we want. For many students, learning is a mystery. We tell them what to do, they try to do it, and then we tell them how they did. I remember students getting nervous after taking one of our tests.

"How did I do?!" I was always a little surprised by this question. Shouldn't they know how they did? Shouldn't they at least have a sense of success or failure? Assessments were a bit like slot machines; students would pull the bar and wait to see what they got, hoping for matching fruit.

Part of the problem—okay, most of the problem—was that we (the teachers) had no idea what we really wanted. Some skills were easy. We knew we needed x number of pages in x font with x spacing; we knew we wanted x number of quotes, x number of paragraphs, and no comma errors; we knew we wanted strong purpose, quality evidence, and insightful analysis—but what did that look like? Well, we knew it when we saw it.

This is not okay. If we want students to meet our targets, they must be able to clearly see them. And in order for us to show them, we need to have a deep and thorough and crystal-clear understanding of these targets ourselves.

Strategy: Benchmark Sheets

The creation of benchmark sheets is one of the most challenging and important instructional endeavors we have taken on. The purpose of a benchmark sheet is to clearly define the progression of learning and offer students examples that show specifically how to improve. By doing this, we also become much clearer about how to instruct the skill in a way that will lead to improvement.

When creating a benchmark sheet for our evidence target, we knew we needed to define some of the words we used in the scale.

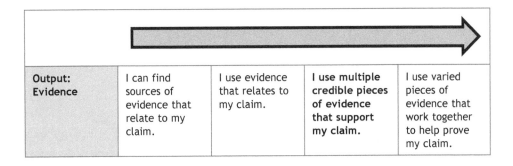

Output: Evidence	I can find sources of evidence that relate to my claim.	I use evidence that relates to my claim.	**I use multiple credible pieces of evidence that support my claim.**	I use varied pieces of evidence that work together to help prove my claim.

We started by defining the words or phrases that were central to success in this skill.

- *Credible*: Evidence can be credible for a variety of reasons. First, consider the source; if the evidence is from a website, is it .com, .org, or .edu? If your source is a person, why is he or she the best voice for your topic? What specific qualifications or degrees or experience does that person have that makes him or her an expert in your topic?

- *Varied Pieces of Evidence*: When choosing evidence, consider the type of evidence (quote from expert, statistics, broad, general, specific, detailed, anecdote, etc.) and the source (primary, secondary, tertiary, video, text, lecture, speech, etc.). When proving a claim or thesis, you want to vary your evidence so that your pieces don't all come from the same source (or type of source) or are not all the same type of evidence.

- *Work Together to Help Prove My Purpose*: This is the toughest part of the target, as you have to really think about how each piece works together to prove your thesis. That means you need to be intentional about placement and explicit in your justification of this placement. Why did you start with the first piece? How does it work with your thesis? What (specifically) makes it the best first piece of evidence?

Also, since we were asking students to use varied pieces of evidence, we thought it was necessary to outline examples of varieties of evidence.

- **Anecdotal:** These are brief stories that someone tells to make or illustrate a point. They are often helpful when filling out a larger story, providing engaging examples, or hooking your audience. Anecdotes often lack credibility, however, so they are best used in conjunction with other types of evidence.

- **First-Person Account:** Many of your interviews will be first-person evidence. This is different than anecdotal because you are hearing from the person who actually experienced what you are claiming or researching. This is a powerful type of evidence but also needs to be paired with more objective types if you are trying to prove a claim or build an argument. First-person accounts are often vivid, believable, and engaging, but they can be incredibly subjective and driven by bias.

- **Experiential:** Throughout your research, you may experience things personally that you want to use as evidence. Like the first-person account, this is great and can be very powerful, but only when used together with less subjective forms of evidence.

- **Research:** There are many types of research, but for the sake of brevity, let's assume a book or online source here. It's important to look at lots of research when trying to convince an audience, even if you don't end up using it in your final product. Research will give you background knowledge to use in your interviews and will help you make sense of the other evidence you come across. When including research in your work, summarize and paraphrase carefully and be sure to cite your sources in order to avoid plagiarism. Also, be sure your research sources are credible and varied.

- **Statistics:** These can be incredibly powerful when used well and used sparingly. Be aware that statistics can be misleading, so make sure you have verified them before using them.

- **Quotes:** Like statistics, these can be powerful or misleading. If you are quoting a person, be sure you are quoting them exactly; if you are quoting a source, be sure that you are choosing the part of the quote that is most relevant and necessary to your story.

- **Other:** Evidence can come from many places, so don't limit yourself to what is listed above. Remember to gather lots of evidence, because the more you have, the more you have to choose from when building your final product.

We also created examples at each level to show what we were expecting.

Creating this benchmark sheet forced us to not only articulate but to also really understand what we wanted when it came to evidence. Once we had come to grips with it ourselves, we were able to teach it much more effectively. And it should come as no surprise that once we knew what we were teaching (in this case, how to effectively use evidence to support a claim) our students were able to not only reach the target more efficiently, but quickly showed us that they could achieve a level of complexity with their thinking that we had rarely seen before.

Benchmark sheets also increased student creativity, which may seem counterintuitive. Sometimes teachers of courses that encourage creativity fear that showing exemplars will limit creativity and lead to mimicry at best, but we have not found that to be true. Showing students what we expect often leads to greater efficiency in learning, which then allows time for innovation. During the practice phase, benchmarks help students match the learning. Just as an art teacher may have students emulate Monet's style or an English teacher may ask students to write as if they were e e cummings, mimicry early in the learning process helps students understand content and skills. When asked to perform for the summative, they can then use what they have practiced to be even more creative or imaginative than our exemplars demonstrated. Over time, we can build a varied set of exemplars at each level that can continue to inspire students to innovate.

Many of the teachers in our district are starting to use benchmark sheets, and those that have loudly sing their praises. Figures 7.5, 7.6, and 7.7 show a few that have been successfully used with students.

FIGURE 7.5 Benchmark Sheet Example 1

Integrated Biology

Name _____ Block _____

Analyzing Data Benchmark Sheet

Analyzing Data: Writing Captions	When given	When given a data set	When given a	In addition
Analyzing Data: Writing Captions *appropriate mathematical calculations (average, difference, range) ^factors that could have impacted the results beyond human error.	When given data with two variables, I can write a statement that describes the relationship between the two variables.	When given a data set with three variables, I can write a statement that describes the relationships among all three *or* I can write a caption that describes the relationship between two of the three variables using specific evidence* from the graph/table.	**When given a data set with three variables, I can explain all of the relationships by stating the trends and supporting them with specific evidence* from the graph/table.**	In addition to the earlier targets, I can pose an explanation for the relationship and any outliers or limitations.^

Once collected, data must be presented in a form that can reveal any patterns and relationships and that allows the results to be communicated to others. Because raw data as such have little meaning, a major practice of scientists is to organize and interpret data through tabulating or statistical analysis. Such analysis can bring out the meaning of data—and their relevance—so that they may be used as evidence. You will be analyzing data in Integrated Biology for the same reason and to show that you understand multiple cause-and-effect relationships.

Scale Descriptors:

Variables: These are the conditions of the experiment that are either changed by the investigator (independent variables) or measured by the investigator (dependent variable).

Trend: This states the relationship between all three variables. Think about it in terms of change. As the independent variables (x-axis or different lines/bars) are changed (e.g., increases, decreases, etc.), how does the dependent variable (y-axis) change (e.g., increase, decrease, remain constant, etc.)? Avoid using the words *go up* and *go down*; instead, use *increase* or *decrease*.

Specific Evidence: What specific numbers or categories can you pull from the graph to provide examples of the relationship between variables?

Mathematical Calculations:

Average. Calculate the average by adding the values for each trial and dividing by the number of trials.

Difference. Calculate the difference by subtracting one value (often averages) from another.

Range. A range represents the highest and lowest values in the trial. For example, if the trials were 3.0, 4.1 and 3.3, the range would be reported as (3.0–4.1).

Limitations: Identifying the limitations of a data set takes into account factors or variables that may not be able to be controlled in the experiment. For example, if we were experimenting with plants and we were unable to water them over a long weekend, that may affect our results. Or if we were watering plants with tap water, we might accidentally be adding other chemicals (e.g., fluoride, chloride, bleach, etc.), which could affect the growth of plants.

Outliers: These are data points that seem to fall outside of the general pattern. For example, if you had 10 plants that were all about 9" tall and one plant that was 15" tall, the later would be an outlier, and you would need to figure out why it was dramatically different.

Possible Explanation: This is where you connect the data with what we have been doing in class. For example, you should be able to figure out why plants watered with salt water grew less than plants watered with plain water, based on what you know about how plants grow (photosynthesis) and what they need to grow (water, sunlight, and carbon dioxide).

Created in collaboration with Jess Lemieux.

FIGURE 7.6   Benchmark Sheet Example 2

Examples: The examples below represent captions at each level of the scale for the following data set.

Frequency (Hz)	Wavelength (m)	Speed (m/s)
20	.8	16
12	1.3	16
4	4	16

1	When given data with two variables, I can write a statement that describes the relationship between two variables.	• When the frequency was low, the wavelength was long. • This table shows the speed, wavelength, and frequency of waves.
2	When given a data set with three variables, I can write a statement that describes the relationships among all three *or* I can write a caption that describes the relationship between two of the three variables using specific evidence* from the graph/table.	• When the frequency was low, the wavelength was long and the speed stayed the same. • When the frequency was low (4Hz), the wavelength was long (4m). When the frequency was high (20Hz), the average wavelength was shorter (0.8m)
3	When given a data set with three variables, I can explain all of the relationships by stating the trends and supporting them with specific evidence* from the graph/table.	• As the frequency of a wave decreases, the wavelength gets longer and the speed remains constant. When the frequency was low (4hz), the average wavelength was long (4m) and the average speed was 16. When the frequency was high (20Hz), the average wavelength was shorter (0.8m) and the speed of the wave was the same (16m/s).
4	In addition to the earlier targets, I can pose an explanation for the relationship and any outliers or limitations.^	• As the frequency of a wave decreases, the wavelength gets longer and the speed remains constant. When the frequency was low (4hz), the average wavelength was long (4m) and the average speed was 16m/s. When the frequency was high (20Hz), the average wavelength was shorter (0.8m) and the speed of the wave was the same (16m/s). The frequency of the

(Continued)

(Continued)

		wave is set by whatever is causing the wave, while the speed of the wave is determined by whatever the wave is traveling in (medium). Wavelength is calculated by dividing the speed by the frequency. Since the medium didn't change, the speed remained constant; but when the frequency changed, the wavelength changed. Although the slinky experiment gives us a general idea about the relationship between amplitude, wavelength, and frequency, there is no quantitative data to use to calculate a relationship. Therefore, we don't know if the relationship is linear or exponential.

Created in collaboration with Jess Lemieux.

FIGURE 7.7   Benchmark Sheet Example 3

Benchmark Sheet: How to Improve a Thesis Target

	1	2	3	4
Output: Purpose	I have a clear thesis/claim with a single idea; the claim requires simple evidence and no analysis to prove.	I have a clear thesis/claim with more than one idea; the claim requires a single type of evidence and limited analysis to prove.	I have a clear thesis/claim with multiple relational ideas; the claim requires multiple types of evidence and substantive analysis to prove.	**I have a clear, complex thesis/claim that includes multiple arguments; the claim requires an organized evidence strategy and analysis that includes inference.**

Writing a thesis (making a claim) is incredibly complex and essential for success on other output targets. Your thesis controls your argument, so a good thesis will lead to logical organization, great evidence, and sophisticated analysis. Conversely, if the claim is not complex, the argument cannot be complex.

We have decided to use basic algebraic relationships to show the difference between the levels. Note the differences between the types of thinking and evidence required to support each level of claim.

Target Level	Math	Thesis/Claim Example	Explanation of Level: Necessary Evidence and Analysis
1	x	Pollard is a leader.	A single idea that requires one piece of evidence and no analysis to prove. It's a fact.
2	$x+y$	Pollard and Chase have different leadership styles.	There are two ideas here, one about Pollard's style and one about Chase's style. While there is a simple relationship (*different*), the evidence is all the same type and does not rely on each other. I would need to find examples of Pollard's style and examples of Chase's style: two separate but equal ideas. The analysis I need would be limited to the individual ideas.

Target Level	Math	Thesis/Claim Example	Explanation of Level: Necessary Evidence and Analysis
3	$x(y)$ or x^y	Pollard's leadership style is more effective than Chase's.	Again, there are two ideas here, one about Pollard and one about Chase. But these ideas are relational because there is a comparison (*more effective*), which will require two categories of evidence for each idea (examples of Pollard's style and examples of his style being effective, examples of Chase's style and examples of his style being ineffective). In addition, this will require a lot of analysis (evaluating each leader's decisions in relation to their individual styles and then proving that one is more effective); the analysis requires interplay between the ideas.
4	$x(y)^z$ or $(x+y)z$	Both Pollard and Chase have effective leadership styles, but the dire circumstances facing the crew call for the first mate's more Machiavellian beliefs.	There are not only multiple ideas here, but there are multiple arguments (two connected claims). In order to prove this claim, I would have to have a multipart system (first, define Pollard and Chase's styles and prove they are both effective; then establish how Chase is more Machiavellian than Pollard; and finally, prove that these practices are more effective, due to the circumstances).

Challenges

Expert Blind Spot: Because most teachers have worked hard over years or decades to become experts in our discipline areas, we can easily fall into the expert blind spot trap when teaching. There are significant differences in how experts (we) and novices (our students) learn new content. Experts have developed conceptual understanding, which means we know how knowledge is organized in our discipline and therefore can connect new content quickly to established patterns or concepts. Novices do not yet have this conceptual understanding; their brains don't have existing structures to connect the new learning to, and therefore, they are much less likely to be able to turn content into usable knowledge. As Jerome Bruner wrote in *The Process of Education* (1960), "Knowledge one has acquired without sufficient structure to tie it together is knowledge that is likely to be forgotten. An unconnected set of facts has a pitiably short half-life in memory" (p. 31). Because we have the "sufficient structures" already, our content makes complete sense to us. We understand why x piece of knowledge is essential to y and how z logically leads to w. In order to be able to back up and instruct skills and content to our novice learners, we need to remember what it was like to not know (and to be blunt, to not care, in many cases). And this is not easy.

Letting Go: Let's face it, many of us became teachers because we are control freaks. Not only do we like knowing the *why*, the *what*, and the *how*, but we also want to be the one in charge of the *why*, the *what*, and the *how*. Standards-based instructional practices still often keep us in charge of the *why* but require us to let go of the *what* and the *how* a bit, to let students take the reins. This is not easy. When students have more control, that means we have less. We won't know exactly what will happen, how long the *what* will take, or where the *what* might lead us in the short run. We may be surprised by how the *how* unfolds, how short or long the *how* takes, or what the *how* uncovers about additional instructional needs. Letting go in the classroom isn't only about letting go of time in the front of the room, it's about letting go of knowing what will happen day to day. It's about not being able to have our lessons planned more than a few days in advance. It's about not being able to set a concrete end date for a unit until we know how the learning is going. None of this is easy for most teachers, but it's essential if learning is our goal.

The Guilt-Free Box

Overwhelmed by all of the intentional moving parts? Wondering how to instruct critical thinking? Worried that you will have to change everything and throw away all of your existing lesson plans? Start small.

- Instead of creating an entire benchmark sheet, focus on a clear explanation and understanding of the 3 to 4. This tends to be the one that kids and parents struggle with and demand the most. So, start by making sure you have that down; the rest will come later.

- Time yourself. Have a student time how long you talk in front of the whole class or time yourself. Record times for a week and then see what you think and begin to respond accordingly (especially if you are talking for over 20% of the class time).

CHAPTER 8

Differentiating by Readiness

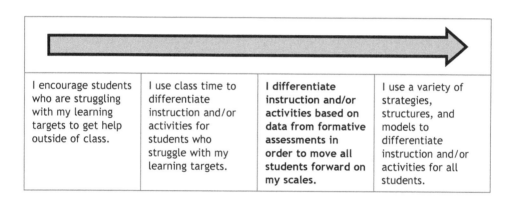

I encourage students who are struggling with my learning targets to get help outside of class.	I use class time to differentiate instruction and/or activities for students who struggle with my learning targets.	**I differentiate instruction and/or activities based on data from formative assessments in order to move all students forward on my scales.**	I use a variety of strategies, structures, and models to differentiate instruction and/or activities for all students.

COMMENTARY AND CONTEXT

Perhaps the single greatest instructional benefit of standards-based learning (SBL) is how effectively it sets us up to differentiate by readiness. When tracking achievement based on tasks (as we did in the traditional teaching model), it's easy to gloss over student differences and cloud our assessment and communication; we can add or subtract points for everything from lateness to neatness to skill demonstration to content knowledge. When planning, instructing, and assessing using learning targets and scales, however, it's nearly impossible to ignore student differences. In a standards-based classroom, we track specific skills (not only general tasks), and so we can no longer confuse a student's neatness with his or her ability to develop a thesis statement. Once we have isolated this skill achievement, we cannot ignore our role (and responsibility) in each student's progress. And so, we must differentiate.

There are many ways to differentiate and many reasons to do so. You can differentiate by interest, tapping into the power of choice and relevance; you can differentiate by learning profile or preference, capitalizing on efficiency; or you can differentiate by readiness, using what we know about learning to challenge all students from where they are. Each of these is valuable. The focus of this chapter, however, is on differentiation by readiness based on formative assessment data.

Differentiating by readiness is not tracking. This is really important to understand, as the research about tracking is clear and disturbing; we do not want to label students or put them in groups that limit their options, damage or falsely inflate their self-esteem, or set unfair expectations for learning. Readiness grouping is not tracking. One main difference is the flexibility that comes from determining needs based on precise learning targets; students in the most advanced group for one skill will not be in that same group for another skill, and students who struggle with a particular skill one week will find themselves in a different group (and with different peers) when focusing on a different skill the following week. Another main difference between readiness grouping and tracking is the timing; tracking is done over long term, while grouping might be used for no more than 30 minutes in a class. Tracking assumes a broad skill strength or deficit (often incorrectly or unfairly), and readiness grouping is based on specific evidence of a precise skill and is therefore much more likely to change and vary in time. We should not group students based on broad categories of skill (i.e., reading, writing, speaking) but rather on specific skills that we have intentionally assessed (i.e., inference in reading, purpose in writing, or projection in speaking).

Differentiating by readiness is often the most efficient and effective way to ensure student progression on a particular skill. When we meet students where they are and provide an appropriate challenge to get them to the next clear target level, they are much more likely to get there. Experiencing success is vital to learning, and when students see that the work they did in differentiated groups led to immediate growth, they will be much more willing to persevere when they struggle. The outcome for the most advanced students is equally as rewarding; we all want to be challenged, and when our achievement is recognized and honored by added complexity rather than additional work, we feel respected as learners. Our role as teachers is to challenge each one of our students; differentiating by readiness not only allows us to do this but demands that we do.

THE PRACTICAL PART

We have developed a template and system that helps teachers both new to and experienced with differentiation become more intentional and efficient in their attempts to help all students progress (see Figure 8.1). As with everything in this book, we encourage you to adapt this to fit your style and needs.

FIGURE 8.1   Differentiation Template

Target and Scale				
Student Groups				
Determining Needs				
Planning and Organizing				

TARGET AND SCALE

Start with a target you are currently working with in class. You will need a scale for the target, preferably a transferable skill scale. As we discovered years ago, trying to differentiate content targets is nearly impossible without throwing more work at some students and less at others. We used to assign our strongest readers an additional book or ask our strongest writers to write ten pages instead of five. We'd find shorter books for our struggling readers and cut page amounts for our struggling writers. What we were doing was raising and lowering the difficulty of the input or output (not the complexity) without actually differentiating our instruction. But if you have a scale that defines multiple levels of skill progression (increasing in complexity), designing multiple tasks becomes much more manageable. Figure 8.2 is a speaking scale with a specific focus on voice and presence. Our summative was a persuasive speech, so we needed to work on multiple elements of speaking; we isolated this skill, as it seemed to have the most variation.

FIGURE 8.2   Example Differentiation of Target and Scale, Student Groups

Differentiating by Readiness in a Standards-Based Classroom				
	→			
Target and Scale: Voice and Presence	I am beginning to use my voice as a presenter.	I have some control over my voice and speak so that I can be heard; I use interrupters (*umms, ahhs, like,* and *yeah*).	**I project my voice with appropriate volume and pace so that my audience can easily understand me; I speak with few interrupters (*umms, ahhs, like,* and *yeah*), and they don't distract from my presentation.**	I use emphasis/ emotion throughout the presentation and vary my pace to support my purpose; I use few or no interrupters and smoothly transition between sentences.
Student Groups				

STUDENT GROUPS

Carefully and intentionally design a formative assessment that will provide data of individual student achievement at all levels of the scale. Sort your student formatives into four piles, each corresponding with a level on the scale. This is a great time to revise the language of your scale if necessary, as seeing student work can often help define the levels of the scale more accurately and clearly. If you do revise the language, remember to let students know that you did. Once you have your student work sorted, enter the student names in the second row of the template. Occasionally, you will have an outlier that does not fit on your scale. Be sure to note this so that you can plan for these students as well.

DETERMINING NEEDS

Now that you have the work sorted, take a look at each pile or evidence of work (in the case of the speaking scale, we made notes on achievement) and look for common misconceptions, patterns, missing ideas, and clear areas of need. Based on your analysis, what does each group need to move up a level? Think about the difference between instructional needs and practice needs. Consider which students would benefit from individual work and which students need group instruction or group work. Looking at the evidence of learning, what is your diagnosis for each level? This is where you plan for the ideal, meaning that you write what each group needs, regardless of logistical difficulties. Figure 8.3 gives an example.

FIGURE 8.3   Example Differentiation of Determining Needs

Determining Needs	These students need more practice/time taking risks in front of an audience; they need to become comfortable enough to want to be heard and understood. **Possibilities to move forward:** • small-group, low-risk activities • same as 2s here—some discussion about nerves	These students are probably nervous. It might make sense to talk with them about this: Why do they get nervous? What's the worst thing that could happen? What do you do if the worst does happen? How can you use your voice as a tool, as a weapon, or persuasively? **Possibilities to move forward:** • discussion about nerves • examples of speeches	These students are using their voices clearly to communicate but are not yet using them to manipulate their audience's emotions or responses. They may not know how to vary the elements or how to do this in a way that increases engagement or meaning. **Possibilities to move forward:** • show examples of speeches/clips with great variance and use of voice • practicing using Little Mr./Little Miss books and varying pace, tone, volume, emphasis, and emotion	Again, these students have more confidence. We might want them to see some of the more sophisticated rhetorical strategies that presenters use and to begin to think about nuances of presenting and speech writing. **Possibilities to move forward:** • show examples of speeches/clips with great variance and use of voice • look at rhetorical strategies

PLANNING AND ORGANIZING

Finally, it's time to determine the best way to organize the differentiated lesson. You may need to compromise a bit, based on the realities of your experience, your particular students, your environment, or your time constraints. But try to get as close to the ideal as possible, as that is what you (the professional) have determined will provide the greatest learning. You may decide to combine a few groups, to split the lesson into multiple days, or to ask a colleague to help with the lesson. Note in Figure 8.4 that we chose to run three groups only for this lesson, as the needs of the two middle groups were similar (and we were worried about the management of four groups in a small space).

FIGURE 8.4   Example Differentiation of Planning and Organizing

Planning and Organizing	**Instruction Needed:** Make sure students know the language of the scale (volume, pace, interrupters). **Activity:** Use a circle discussion (teacher led); start with a discussion on nerves and lead into low-risk individual speaking. **Outcome:** Students are prepared to speak their quote in front of class.	**Instruction Needed:** How do I use volume and pace in my speaking? Why would this matter? What is inflection? **Activity:** Discuss volume, pace, emphasis, and emotion. Use the teacher-led activity to practice each skill using Little Miss/Little Mr. books. **Outcome:** Students are prepared to speak their quote in front of class using volume and pacing, inflection, and emotion.	**Instruction Needed:** What is rhetoric? What are some common rhetorical strategies? **Activity:** Watch the *Miracle* speech and analyze pace, volume, inflection, emotion, movement, and gestures. **Outcome:** Students are prepared to speak their quote in front of the class, a la *Miracle*.

Figure 8.5 shows another example of a completed differentiation template from an eighth-grade science class working on an evidence target.

FIGURE 8.5 Example of a Completed Differentiation Template

Target and Scale: Evidence	I can use my own ideas to support my claim.	I can select and use evidence that relates to my claim.	**I can select and use multiple credible pieces of evidence that support my claim.**	I can select and use credible, varied, and compelling pieces of evidence that work together to support my claim.
Student Groups	Adam B. Sven M. Jeff E.	Josh B. Jen M. Tammi C. Sarah C. Connie M. Katherine R. Ken C. Scotty S.	Monica C. Jessie L. Don A. Molly P. Brad B. Tim B. Jen G. Sharon C. Peter R. Allegra M. Sara A.	John G. Dave C. Bob R. Sage B. Jess H.
Determining Needs	1. Identify what results from the investigation are related to the claim. 2. Select numerical values whenever possible.	1. Explicitly address the dependent variable when selecting evidence and explain how it has varied in response to the independent variable. 2. Give specific numerical values as evidence (either raw data points or results of data analysis). 3. Interpret the data/data analysis presented and give inferences.	1. Explicitly tell the reader how pieces of evidence work together to support the author's claim. 2. Present evidence sequentially to help show connections between the pieces of evidence.	These students would benefit from seeing professional scientific analysis in order to explore how to raise the sophistication of their connections and arguments.
Planning and Organizing	**Direct Instruction:** Define terms (*relate, support, work together*). **Group Tile Activity:** Students sort evidence into categories (doesn't relate/relates/supports). Students individually revise their work.	**Direct Instruction:** Define/review terms (*dependent/independent variable*). **Group Activity:** Look at exemplars from a different investigation at Level 3. Identify dependent and independent variables; highlight analysis and inferences. Students individually revise their work.	**Direct Instruction:** None. **Group Activity:** Look at a template/flowchart using evidence from an earlier investigation; sequence and justify the evidence based on exemplars. Students individually revise their work.	**Direct Instruction:** None. **Individual Activity:** Read selected writings from the *American Journal of Medicine*, looking for the use of evidence. **Group Activity:** Discuss the individual selections and determine three steps students could take to improve their argument.

One of the most difficult aspects of differentiation is the management of multiple groups with different needs. Many teachers struggle to organize and facilitate multiple activities within a single classroom. They say that they could never trust fifth graders, eighth graders, or twelfth graders to work effectively without the teacher right there. This isn't true at any grade level. The key to successful management is building the habits and systems that will encourage effective work. This may take some practice and some trial and error, but it won't be long before you figure out the types of instruction and activities that work best for your community (or your teaching style). Anchor tasks, stations, task sheets, and general classroom habits and systems can help make the difference between time well spent and total chaos.

- **Anchor Tasks:** Establishing an ongoing, high-engagement, personalized anchor task early in the year is one of the most effective strategies for management of differentiation. In our classes for the last five years, we used blogs as our anchors, working with students early in the year to establish their digital presence and the routines and individual focus we came to rely on as the year progressed. It became common and easy for us to tell groups of students to work on their blogs while we spent some time with students who needed new instruction, extra guided practice, or additional challenge with our learning targets. Blogs and websites are inherently engaging and relevant to most students, particularly if we don't control every aspect of them; in addition, they allow students to push their thinking about content, practice writing, and learn a valuable and real-world media skill. Many teachers now incorporate time into their classes (such as 20% of the classroom time) for individual pursuits. Once the routines and structures are in place, this time can act as a great anchor as well. The key to this is ensuring that you aren't always pulling the same students from their topics; it's important that all students get to experience independent learning.

- **Stations:** This classic management technique for differentiation is often abandoned by teachers who have a few bad experiences early in the year. Like anything, this strategy takes time and practice, but eventually, and with good planning, students can be doing multiple things in multiple places, allowing the teacher to target instruction with small groups. It's important that each station has a clearly defined purpose and task and that students know what to do if they get stuck or confused. Also, physical layout can be the key to success with stations, so take the time to set the room up, even if this takes time out of your class. Once routines are set, students can help with the movement of furniture, which will save time and encourage movement and teamwork.

- **Task Sheets:** Task sheets are more than written directions, and they can be instrumental in ensuring clarity of purpose and focus when running multiple activities in the same room. An effective task sheet includes the scale that you're focusing on, the purpose of the task, the desired outcome, and specific instructions. By color coding these, or coding in some other way, it's easy to prioritize your focus with students and sort student work after the class. See Chapter 6 for specific examples of task sheets.

- **Harbor Day**: A few colleagues shared this strategy that they have adapted from a neighboring district. Every few weeks they declare a Harbor Day, a class when the ships (students) return to the harbor to rest, refuel, repair, and reprovision. This allows the teachers the space and time to work with small groups of students that they have been unable to reach during their regular classes. Students appreciate the Harbor Days and the majority use the time to think, reflect, catch up, or push their thinking. Imagine if teachers were provided a day at school without students each quarter to use as we needed. Amazing thought, right? Too often, we fill every minute of every class for our students, but the benefits from regular Harbor Days far outweigh the loss of new instructional time.

Challenges

Planning Time: Effective readiness-based differentiated lessons can take time to plan and prepare. Unlike regular lessons or activities that may involve a single set of materials, a single task sheet, and a single instructional plan, differentiated lessons may require multiple high-prep plans. Full-time teachers never have enough time as it is, so doubling or tripling planning time for a single class can seem overwhelming at best and impossible at worst. This is why high-prep differentiation cannot happen daily or even weekly. The key is to choose your differentiation wisely, making sure that your prep is leading to significant learning and that the skill you are differentiating is central to success in your class.

Not all differentiated lessons need to be high prep, however. There are simple systems and templates that you can begin to develop that can be used with almost any skill or content. For example, starting class every day with a 20-minute station activity can set you up for easy prep differentiation. Who is at which station can vary based on the students you need to work with, and having routines built in at the student-led stations means little to no prep is needed. Also, we do not usually have to wait until we have formatively assessed to plan for differentiation. We may not know yet which students will need which instruction, but we can be pretty sure what each level of instruction will need to be.

Finally, planning time can increase if we can decrease our time somewhere else, namely, our time spent grading student work. Before becoming standards-based, the majority of our time was spent grading, scoring, or commenting on student work; now, the vast majority is spent planning.

Community: One of the biggest obstacles to differentiating by readiness is teacher fear. And it's a specific fear—the fear of the student who will say, "Why am I in the dummy group?" This very well could happen, though the words may vary, so being ready early in the year to address the question is important. If your class has already built an environment of learning with a growth mindset—which takes time, intentional systems, and hard work—then this becomes easier to answer. This also becomes easier to address when you are grouping often and in a variety of ways—not only by readiness. Talking to students about flexibility and the need for multiple types of groupings based on needs should happen early and often in your classes and, hopefully, all over your school. Soon, it will become so second nature that students will start asking for groupings based on their own understanding of their needs. It's beautiful when this happens, and you'll know you have become an effective differentiator.

The Guilt-Free Box

Overwhelmed by the thought of planning one lesson per class let alone three or four? Wondering how to manage multiple groups in a small room with only one of you? Worried about what your students will say if you put them in groups based on specific needs? Start small.

- Decide to create one differentiated lesson in your next unit. Use the template to help plan it and ask for lots of management help from wherever you can find it. You might be surprised who is willing to work with one of your groups— ask your principal (and if you are a principal reading this, send out an e-mail immediately offering to help with groups!), ask a colleague (and offer a trade of time), or ask a few older students (if you are in middle school, see if a few high school students can come over for a bit).

- Start with two groups, even if your formative data show you need three or four. Any differentiation is better than no differentiation, so allow yourself to take a first step.

Monitor and Communicate Learning

Grading practices and decisions have always been intensely personal, and it's not until we start publicly questioning these that we realize how sensitive the topic can be. Teachers may see new grading best practices as a direct challenge to their professionalism and as a judgement on past (or current) practices. Families and students may see new grading practices as an unfair change in the rules, as an experiment with their children's futures, or as a direct affront to their own educations. Do not underestimate the difficulty of these changes, despite the overwhelming research that supports them. We messed this up early in our process by not intentionally ensuring enough safe spaces to talk, enough time to privately reflect, and enough structures to build confidence and beliefs about the changing purpose of grading. Being purposeful and intentional about communication, whether in your classroom or as a school, will help make the transition possible and positive for all involved.

[GLOSSARY OF KEY TERMS]

Score: When we use the term *score*, we are talking about where a student falls on a learning scale. Scores can be formative or summative, and they are shorthand for the language within the corresponding box on the scale. At our school, we use a 1-4 scoring system, but others may use symbols or words. Some teachers use the term *mark* to mean the same thing.

Grade: At our high school, we are still required to give a composite letter grade (A-F) at the end of each semester. Currently, this letter grade is determined by combining a student's scores on different learning targets (yes, it feels dirty to us and is something we hope to get away from soon).

FURTHER EXPLORATION

Ken O'Connor: Absolutely the first books you should read if you want to change to more learning-friendly grading practices are *How to Grade for Learning: Linking Grades to Standards* (2018) and *A Repair Kit for Grading: 15 Fixes for Broken Grades* (2011). Both are incredibly clear, practical guides for teachers and schools who want to ensure that their grading practices are fair, are accurate, and support what we know about the brain and learning. One of our favorite aspects of *A Repair Kit* is how easy it is to use with full faculties; the chapters can be read individually based on need or interest, which makes it a valuable resource for every educational library.

Thomas Guskey: While reading just about anything by Thomas Guskey will improve your teaching, his short, easy-to-read book about grading, *On Your Mark: Challenging the Conventions of Grading and Reporting* (2015), offers a nice balance of philosophical and practical advice. His chapter on establishing the purpose of grading is particularly important, and had we read it three years earlier than we did, it could have prevented a great deal of stress and saved us all a lot of time. We like to think that our mistakes made us stronger, but we're probably only saying that to rationalize the drinking and the tears.

Doug Reeves: No education library would be complete without Doug Reeves. He has so many great books about leadership, but for this section, we suggest *FAST Grading: A Guide to Implementing Best Practices* (2016). This clear, practical guide walks readers through common mistakes, best-practice strategies, and how to implement significant and powerful change. His expertise and knowledge about grading reform will help you come up with effective systems, whether for your own classroom or for the entire district.

Jim Knight: While mostly known for his exceptional work on instructional coaching, Jim Knight is a master of communication. His book *Better Conversations* (2016) will improve every relationship in your life. Really. He teaches how to listen better, how to have difficult discussions, and how to be aware of your own challenges and biases when communicating. It's a super practical book as well, with concrete suggestions about how to get started. Whether you want to be more intentional in your communication with students, parents, colleagues, or family members, this is the guy to look to.

The Heath Brothers: While not books about education, both *Made to Stick* (2008) and *Switch* (2010) by Chip and Dan Heath will help guide messaging during tricky transitions. The second, *Switch: How to Change Things When Change Is Hard*, discusses the challenges of change—which we all know—and provides clear and clever ways to navigate those changes—which we all need. We found this book instrumental in how we planned for the changes within our school and community—and we wish we had read it even sooner so that we could have avoided some of the early pitfalls caused by out-of-control elephants and eager riders (which will make sense after you read the book!).

Tammy Heflebower, Jan K Hoegh, and Phil Warrick: Even though we don't focus on leadership for schoolwide change, it's worth including *A School Leader's Guide to Standards-Based Grading* (2014) on our list of suggestions. Leaders attempting to guide the transformation to a standards-based school should probably read all of these books, but as we have discovered over the past eight years, school leaders have other balls they must keep in the air and may not have time to read everything. Heflebower, Hoegh, and Warrick's book provides a concise overview of the steps involved in transformation, and though our process looked a little different and our path veered at times from their suggestions, it's a great book to help support significant change.

CHAPTER 9

Monitoring and Grading Learning

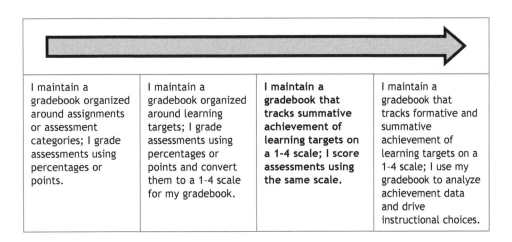

I maintain a gradebook organized around assignments or assessment categories; I grade assessments using percentages or points.	I maintain a gradebook organized around learning targets; I grade assessments using percentages or points and convert them to a 1-4 scale for my gradebook.	**I maintain a gradebook that tracks summative achievement of learning targets on a 1-4 scale; I score assessments using the same scale.**	I maintain a gradebook that tracks formative and summative achievement of learning targets on a 1-4 scale; I use my gradebook to analyze achievement data and drive instructional choices.

COMMENTARY AND CONTEXT

One of the most significant and impactful changes a teacher can make is changing the gradebook. It may seem silly, but the simple act of changing what and how we record information can lead to significant changes in instruction and assessment. If you Google images of gradebooks from the early 19th century, you will find the same gradebook layout that the majority of current teachers still use. The students are lined up down the left side of the page (whether on paper or online) and across the top are the assignments in the order we have assigned them. In each box is a grade, mark, or score of some sort, summarizing how students did on that assignment. Here's what we loved about that gradebook:

- **It Was Familiar.** This is how we were graded, how we watched our cooperating teachers grade while student teaching, and how we tracked student achievement throughout the majority of our careers. I still remember getting my first real gradebook. It was green. I bought a set of colored pencils to go with it, planning to color code. I spent hours setting it up, carefully writing in my first-ever class lists. I loved that thing.

- **It Was Simple.** Students down the left, assignments across the top, one number in each box. Simple. Neat. At the end of the unit or quarter or semester, I would add up all the numbers and divide by the total number of possible points. Sometimes I would round up. Sometimes I wouldn't. Easy. Clear. Completely objective. (I know, I know . . . but that's the way it seemed at the time.)

- **It Was the Last Word.** Because of my gradebook, I didn't have to think much when it came time for parent conferences or report cards or phone calls. The gradebook did my thinking. Why does Carl have a B-? Let me look. Oh. He has two zeroes. Is there anything Jessie can do to bring her grade up to an A- so she can be on high honors? Let me look. Yes, she didn't do well on her Macbeth test, so maybe she should get a tutor to help with test anxiety. Why did Tim fail the first quarter? Let me look. Right. He didn't do any of his homework assignments. Yes, I know he did well on the test, but look right here: seven zeroes on his homework assignments.

A standards-based gradebook focuses on learning, making the target king rather than the task. Whereas the traditional gradebook was organized by assignment (or in some cases, categories, which we will address later), the new gradebook is organized by the skills we want students to master over time. That means our gradebook needs to allow for multiple attempts at learning while also, ideally, still documenting the assessment that drove that learning. Because many assessments measure multiple targets, our gradebook needs to be flexible enough to record multiple data points for the same assessment over multiple skills. Goodbye simple green gradebook that I loved so much. Hello multidimensional, color-coded, online gradebook that supports what we know about learning!

Once you have chosen a gradebook that supports learning, changing grading practices becomes much easier. As we wrote in our introduction, this book is not about standards-based grading (SBG), so we are going to only focus on a few elements of SBG in this chapter. Instead, we will focus on a few significant areas of change in grading and tracking practices that we think have been the most foundational in our own shift.

Before we get into the practical part, we want to address the purpose of the gradebook and how that has changed over time and in a standards-based classroom. The gradebook used to be only for the teacher. In my first 15 years of teaching, no one but me looked at my gradebook, even when we switched to a software-based program. It was private and personal. The decisions I made about how to grade, how many points to make an assignment, what types of assessments to include—all of these were determined by me and controlled by me. When schools began using online gradebooks with portals, the purpose began to change a bit. While my gradebook was still private, there was now a public view of it as well where parents and students could see real-time grade changes and updates and missing work. Students and parents could now count points, chase grades, and question daily entries. Some teachers loved this. Others dreaded having to update the portal a given number of times per week.

A standards-based gradebook is as much for the learner as it is for the teacher. The gradebook should be a transparent system that tracks progress, documents achievement, and helps both the teachers and the learners plan next steps. If your school has an online portal for families, then your gradebook becomes even more transparent, with your learning targets on display. Since it is our job to ensure learning for all students, our success or failure is also on display; families can see how many times we have assessed specific skills, the type of assignments we are using to gather information, and whether their child is growing over time during our class. In some cases, depending on the gradebook settings, this information is all available to colleagues as well as they track learning for their advisees or homeroom students. Transparency in learning is great, but it can be scary for teachers who are not used to showing the behind-the-scenes view of their grading practices.

Changing grading practices can be intensely personal for teachers, students, and parents. The more purposeful and intentional we can be about our decisions and the more consistency there is across the school system, the easier it will be for students, parents, and teachers to support the changes that will improve learning.

The Practical Part

You're ready to change your grading practices but don't know where to start. We are going to provide a few simple (okay, nothing about this is simple) steps to take in conjunction with reading everything you can by Wormeli, Guskey, and O'Connor.

FLIP YOUR GRADEBOOK

If you have an online SBG option, that's great. It will make life easier, particularly if it was designed specifically for SBG rather than having multiple options. If you don't, that's okay. Some grading programs offer free versions for individual teachers (JumpRope, for example, offers a simple, clear, free version that we used for two years early in our journey) or you can create your own spreadsheet. Some of our teachers preferred making paper spreadsheets early on, with space for multiple practice opportunities per target.

Whichever direction you decide to go, make sure you have flipped the gradebook to track learning rather than doing. In addition to the names of the students, the most prominent aspect of your gradebook will be your learning targets. Every time you gather evidence from a student, you will enter a score (we use 1–4, but it may be any designation your school uses) not for the assessment but for the specific learning target the assessment provided evidence for. This means that a single assessment may provide multiple scores. Your gradebook will also need to be able to track growth over time in each of the learning targets, so if you are creating your own, you will need to leave space for multiple scores in the same target.

Different teachers and schools have different policies regarding the determination of a final score for each target at the end of a period of learning. Here are a few options and our thoughts on each. You will notice that averaging is not one of the options listed, as we should never average within the same skill; how a student did early in the learning should not be averaged equally with their current ability, as it skews the data. When choosing a method, remember that our responsibility is to communicate the most accurate evidence of achievement possible at the time of the communication.

- **Most Recent:** As it sounds, this method takes the most recent score entered for that learning target as the final score at the end of a period of learning. The assumption here is that the teacher has intentionally designed the last assessment to capture the most accurate information about learning. The downfall of this method is that it requires the teacher to pay close attention to the data from that last assessment, because if the score does not match what we know about this student's achievement or ability, then we may need to reassess. (Some thinkers/practitioners have started using *more recent* instead of *most recent* for this reason. The goal is to be accurate, and if the most recent evidence is not accurate for some reason, then looking to previous evidence may be necessary.)

- **Decaying Average or Power Law:** Both of these methods put more weight on the most recent assessments, which is great, but they still take into account the journey to the most recent. Decaying average sets a percentage by which the average decays over time, and power law (designed by Marzano labs) uses a complex algorithm to predict future success based on patterns and trends in the learning. We have found that both are very difficult to explain to students and families, and they still include formative learning, which is philosophically difficult to reconcile if we believe that a student's current achievement should be the most accurate.

- **Mode:** The difference between mean and mode can be significant when looking at multiple data points. The mean is the average, which is similar to what many of us did in the traditional grading system. The problem with the mean or average is it's easy to distort accuracy with outliers, and it does not tell the story of growth. While mode also fails to tell an accurate story of growth, it is based on patterns of achievement, so it can be more accurate than mean. If there are no consistent patterns, however, the mode cannot be calculated, which makes it tough if we do not have enough data points to make the patterns occur.

- **Final Rating**: A final rating method can be set in some grading programs, requiring the teacher to enter a final score. The downfall of this method is it will take a significant amount of time for teachers to enter a final score for every student on every learning target at the end of a period of learning. But what we love about this method is that it requires the teachers to determine the score rather than allowing a program to calculate the score. When done well, final rating means that the professional will look at the body of evidence for each target and then, using what they know about the student and the learning, determine the most accurate score. When done poorly, however, final rating can allow teachers to ignore evidence and enter a score based on nonacademic factors, or in schools that require a conversion to a composite letter grade or GPA, teachers may fudge scores to equal a desired letter grade.

Regardless of the calculation method you (or your school) chooses, the most important thing to remember is that the teacher is the professional. We have the responsibility to have the final score for a period of learning accurately communicate what that student understands and can do, and if the method we use gets in the way of that accuracy—and we have evidence to support that—we need to have a way to make the score match the learning.

CHANGE YOUR LANGUAGE

Once you have flipped your gradebook, it's time to change the language you use to talk about assessing. In a traditional system, everything is graded. We grade homework, we grade quizzes, we grade group work, we grade assessments, and we end up with a final grade. We strongly suggest that you stop using the word *grade* unless you mean an actual summary letter grade that many standards-based schools still have to end up with once or twice a year. Instead of the word *grade*, consider using *score* or *mark* and make sure that all parties understand the difference. When using a 1–4 scale, use the word *assess* to describe the act of looking at work compared to a scale and the word *score* to talk about where the student falls on the scale. For example, rather than telling students that I am going to grade their summatives and let them know what their grades are on the assessment, I would tell students I am assessing their work and will provide scores using the scales. When a student asks what her grade is on an assessment, let her know there are no grades on individual assessments, only scores meant to show current achievement against descriptors. If we are forced to convert scores to grades, hold off as long as possible, making grades come at the end only. This change will take time for teachers, students, and parents, but being careful about our language can help ease the transition to a new way of thinking.

CHANGE YOUR SCORING

In addition to changing the language concerning grading and scoring, we need to change how we score assessments. Our suggestion is this: Throw away all of your old assessments and start from scratch. We know this won't be a popular suggestion, but it's too easy to fall back on previous (and comfortable) practices when using previous (and comfortable) assessments. The biggest change in scoring comes as a result of needing to look at student work as a body of evidence of learning on specific targets rather than a series of points or right or wrong answers. If you have a quiz you have always loved that was 10 questions long and worth 20 points, it's easy to want to score it by marking wrong answers and adding up the pluses or minuses. As we talked about in the assessment chapters, quizzes and tests (any assessments, for that matter) should be organized in a way that gives us evidence of whatever skill or skills we are assessing, and the determination of the score on each target has nothing to do with the number right or wrong or how many points were gained or lost. Many teachers hang onto point scoring, relying on some sort of conversion method to get from a 12/20 to a 60% to a score of 2. This ignores the complexity of learning and communicates false information about what a student understands and can do. We suggest taking the numbers off all items on quizzes and tests as a starting point and avoiding marking assessments using checks, pluses, minuses, or any other notation that will encourage you to add or subtract points. If we keep doing what we have been doing and convert to a new system, then students will continue to play by the rules of the old system, leading to higher confusion and slower change.

DON'T TRACK EVERYTHING

One teacher recently told us that the biggest change for her in the transition to SBG was letting go of grading everything. She said that in her old system—which lasted 15 years—if it moved, she graded it. She always believed that grading everything showed students she was paying attention and motivated them to do the work. She graded homework, group work, class work, extra credit, behavior, big tests, little tests, exit cards, notes—you get the picture. Everything. Her gradebook was color coded and fat. While difficult at first, letting go of this false control and realizing that learning will happen even if (and even more if) we aren't scoring every attempt changed the way this teacher interacted with her classes. Her students began to take more risks, ask better questions, and learn more efficiently.

Just because our students do something doesn't mean we have to score it, and just because we assign something doesn't mean we have to record it. The only scores we enter in our gradebook now are ones that we believe in completely. This means that they are from tasks that are done in class and individually. While we may provide feedback on other work, we do not score it or record it formally. Some teachers have informal ways of recording compliance (Did they do it or not?), but if we score everything we judge everything, and if we judge everything, we risk losing the culture of learning that is central to standards-based learning (SBL) communities.

INFLUENCE WHAT YOU CAN AND COMPROMISE IN ORDER TO MOVE FORWARD

While you may have no direct control over how your school formally reports learning through online portals, report cards, or transcripts, do whatever you can to influence the transformation of these systems and documents. Once you have transitioned to a standards-based class, you will begin to run into systems and structures that contradict what you know about learning but that are beyond your sphere of influence. So, start now and find ways to have some influence. This may mean joining committees, forming discussion groups, or finding the decision makers in your system. Find examples of gradebooks or report cards or transcripts that provide a place to start; sometimes pointing out the contradictions without offering potential solutions can lead to greater dissonance.

Challenges

Guilt for Past Practice: Giving up what's familiar is not easy, and the traditional gradebook can be one of the hardest things to let go of. While comfort and simplicity add to the difficulty, the most significant loss comes from the implications of the change: If we admit that how we were tracking and reporting needs to change, then we must also come to terms with what we did to students for so many years. There's a lot of guilt in changing the gradebook. What we used to do with grading is wrong. But at the time, we didn't know that; now we do. So, if we keep doing what we know is wrong, we are culpable. Students failed our classes because of zeroes on a 100-point scale. That's a big deal. Because of our grading practices, it's possible that students were kept out of other classes, opportunities, or colleges where they would have been incredibly successful. Because of our grading practices, it's possible that students thought they weren't capable, when in reality, they had undeveloped habits of learning. Because of our grading practices, it's possible that students had inflated views of their skills and then failed out of college. We're saying *possible* to let ourselves off the hook a bit. The reality is that all of that is true, and we can still see the faces represented by those zeroes or extra credit points or Fs on the final report card. That's guilt, and it is not comfortable to live with, but we can either choose to defend old practices in order to sleep better, or we can do everything we can to make it better from now on.

Community: Change may need to be incremental, particularly when dealing with the community. For example, even if your teachers believe that converting to a letter grade at the end of a period of learning is meaningless at best and damaging at worst, it may be a necessary step for the community and for colleges; in addition, making this compromise may allow your school to get better at the practices that are essential to successful implementation of SBL, as families and colleges can hang onto what's the same (a grade at the end) while getting used to what's different (everything else). This is the same for the transcript as well. Even though we may believe strongly that the transcript needs to change immediately to reflect learning, maintaining a more traditional transcript for a few years may allow you the space your school needs to figure out what exactly you want to communicate and how you will do that in a way that does not put your students at a disadvantage. Ultimately, our gradebooks, our report cards, and our transcripts need to tell a more accurate and comprehensive story of learning, but it may take some time and strategic energy to make those changes happen.

The Guilt-Free Box

Overwhelmed by the idea of giving up your gradebook? Wondering how parents and students will respond to your changes? Worried that you might do something wrong? Start small.

- Start by lowering the percentage of weight you give anything other than summative data. The more you can rely on the most recent evidence of learning, the more accurate your grades will be.

- If you currently work in a total-points system, start recording work in categories (summative, formative/practice, habits). While you will eventually stop counting the latter two categories in your academic grade, the separation alone can be a great way to start seeing patterns in learning and communicating relationships between practice and achievement.

CHAPTER 10

Communicating With Families

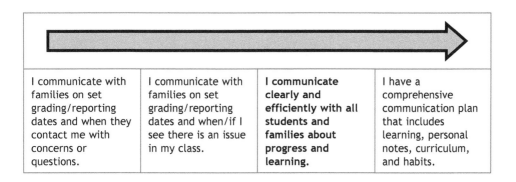

I communicate with families on set grading/reporting dates and when they contact me with concerns or questions.	I communicate with families on set grading/reporting dates and when/if I see there is an issue in my class.	**I communicate clearly and efficiently with all students and families about progress and learning.**	I have a comprehensive communication plan that includes learning, personal notes, curriculum, and habits.

COMMENTARY AND CONTEXT

One of the mistakes we made early on in our transition to standards-based grading (SBG) and reporting was our communication with parents. Because we understood our students' learning so much better than we had in the past, we assumed that reporting that learning to parents would not only help them understand the benefits of a standards-based system, but it would also help them see that we were intentionally addressing both strengths and struggles. After a quarter of great learning and tracking and assessing, we sent detailed standards-based reports home with a key and a brief explanation. We waited for the praise to roll in.

What we forgot, however, was that most parents really want one thing above all else. *They want to know we care about their kids.* Yes, most also want to know if they are being decent human beings, if they are getting their work done, where they are struggling and where they are excelling, and if we have a plan for their learning, but if we know their kids well enough to appreciate the quirks, understand the contradictions, and ultimately enjoy the people they have raised, then parents are usually happy. Our mistake was showing that we knew their students academically without taking the time to show we knew—and liked—them as people as well.

Having a comprehensive communication plan is vital in all classrooms but maybe even more so as we transition to standards-based learning. The shift to a completely new method of teaching and grading can be a difficult change for students and parents; forgetting to communicate what we often do best—which is getting to know our students—can make the transition even harder. Initially, tracking and reporting learning can take a lot of time for teachers, particularly if they are learning a new gradebook tool or using technology differently for the first time; the idea of communicating in *addition* to standards-based reporting can cause stress and force teachers to steal time from other important tasks, such as planning or assessing. Even so, it's an essential part of the transition that can make the difference between class-wide and schoolwide implementation success or failure.

THE PRACTICAL PART

THE PLAN

A comprehensive classroom communication plan has multiple purposes, which overlap at times. We have separated them here, but you'll notice that some of the strategies cross parts, making the communication more efficient. Depending on your teaching situation and the number of students, you may need to adjust ideas to fit your context, and you and your colleagues may have other tried-and-true strategies to add to these lists.

PERSONAL CONNECTIONS

Parents want to know you care about their kid. This means occasionally communicating about specific personal interactions, needs, successes, or other relevant updates.

- **Personal E-mails:** One teacher takes 20 minutes every Friday afternoon to send personal e-mails. She keeps a list of students and checks off when she e-mails their families. The e-mails are short and positive—one nice thing that the student did that week. She can usually get through ten students each week, though she says she tries to send one positive e-mail to each family within the first month.

- **Postcards or Notes Home:** Like e-mails, this is a great way to quickly connect. One teacher gets a set of mailing labels printed at the beginning of the year and pre-labels postcards (generic ones that the school prints). She keeps these next to her computer and tries to send one a day.

- **Parent Conferences:** This is a common way to make personal connections, and teachers we talked to recommend always starting and ending the conferences with positive personal stories or observations.

- **Individual Comments on Standards-Based Reports** (at end of unit, in the portal, or at reporting time): Most SBG and reporting tools allow teachers to enter individual comments. While this can take extra time, a few positive and personal words can go a long way to showing parents that you know their kids and care about their success.

CURRICULUM

Parents want to know what you're doing in class. Letting them know the content you are using to practice important skills can help them feel connected to their kids and can also give them ideas for conversations at home. If your standards are mostly skill based, then communicating about content becomes even more important, as your reporting system may not include the rich, engaging choices you and the students are making about content. Some parents are really interested in the curriculum while others only want to know that there is a curriculum, so it's important to find a balance—consider a system that provides layers of detail that parents can access if they choose.

- **Class and/or Team Blogs or Websites:** While it can be time consuming to keep up a blog or website, many teachers are turning to their students to help, providing a relevant anchor task and another way to work on skills and collaboration. One teacher assigns small writing teams to the task each week, providing guidelines for updates, a chance to include photos, and practice at asking and responding to questions. Another teacher updates his website each unit, providing detailed descriptions of what they will be studying, links to additional videos and related TED talks, and a calendar of summative assessments. In order to ensure that the parents see these updates, he sends a group e-mail to the parents.

- **Google Classroom or Other Learning Management System** (LMS): Many teachers use an LMS to organize tasks and assignments for students, and these can be used with parents as well. Parents can have access to their students' sites, and some teachers set up views for parents within the system as well.

- **Common Blurb on Top of Standards-Based Reports**: Most reporting tools allow teachers to write and post a common message for parents and families. This is an efficient way to provide an overview of the curriculum but should not take the place of more detailed communication for parents who want it.

- **Weekly E-mails From Students to Parents:** This is one of our favorites and can be used for a variety of purposes. One team of teachers has their students write to their families every Friday. They carve out 30 minutes to reflect on the week in a variety of categories, including content, habits, skills, and questions. The students cc their homeroom teachers, and the teachers have set up the e-mails to go directly into a folder (so they don't fill up their inboxes!). The expectation is that this is communication between the student and family, but the teachers can monitor what's being communicated, if necessary. Parents have loved this, and often reply to their kids. (Parents are told that teachers will not reply to these e-mails!)

Figure 10.1 shows an e-mail that a fifth-grade student wrote to her mom.

FIGURE 10.1   Weekly E-mail Example 1

Dear Mom,

The first week of school was awesome! Fifth grade is so much more fun than elementary school. We eat when we want and we get to use locks on our lockers and we go from class to class! This is also the first year we get to try out for band and pick what instrument we want to play. I want to play the tuba!

This week we focused on our schoolwide expectations. These are

- taking care of ourselves
- taking care of others
- taking care of this place

We played games and wrote paragraphs and learned about these expectations. We also got to know each other since there are some new kids this year. The teachers went over our schedule and told us to bring home a copy to keep there. We also learned that everyone can learn even when things are hard. In ELA, we learned what it means to pick a "just right" book. In math we are supposed to talk to our parents about when they use math at home and we learned there is no such thing as a math person.

I can't wait for next week! I'm so excited for the weekend.

Sincerely,
Katie

Figure 10.2 is the response from Katie's mom:

FIGURE 10.2   Weekly E-Mail Example 2

Your email made me so so happy! I often wish I knew more about what you do while you're at school. When you were little I used to know every little detail about your day, but now that you are getting older, you don't like to talk about it as much. I love knowing what you are learning and what you are doing. This email made me feel very connected to you, Katie, and I really appreciate that you wrote it.

I love you so much.

Mom

HABITS AND BEHAVIORS

Parents want to know their kid is doing what they're supposed to be doing, and what to do (or what you're doing) if they're not. Many parents get in the habit of checking online portals for completion, which can cause misunderstandings and stress when they are not accurate or updated regularly. Constant checking such as this can lead to a much greater focus on compliance than on learning, so it's important to develop a system that allows accountability and provides necessary information without distracting from what is most important.

- **Weekly E-mails From Students to Parents:** Getting students to keep track of their own work completion can help them practice positive executive functioning skills. Having students include a to-do list in their weekly e-mail keeps parents informed and prevents having to communicate this in other ways. Early in the year, this may require more organization on the teacher's part (ensuring the lists are accurate), but as time goes on, there will only be a handful of students who need continued guidance (and this is okay—students' executive functioning skills develop at different rates through adolescence). These e-mails are also a great place to ask students to reflect on their behaviors or habits for the week—providing guiding questions can be helpful. One teacher we know also has a few e-mail templates for students who need more structure, with questions already entered.

- **Weekly Contact From Core Teachers:** Teachers who work on a team can collaborate on this type of communication. One team we work with has four teachers and 80 middle school students. They meet once a week to formally talk about students, and during this time, they create a Google Doc list of any significant habits/behaviors or missing work issues that need to be communicated to parents. The core teacher (homeroom teacher) then writes e-mails home to the students on their list that need communication. They found this system to be effective and quickly realized that they did not need to e-mail home every time a student missed an assignment—they were able to coordinate with each other to use school time to address most issues, and those that couldn't be resolved could then be communicated.

- **Summary Habits Scores in Standards-Based Reports:** It's the teacher's job to improve problem habits and behaviors, not only to report them, so we strongly suggest using the formal reporting system for summative habit scores only—and combining this with personal comments and follow-up communication as necessary.

LEARNING

Finally, parents do also want to know how their kid is progressing in skills—where they excel and where they struggle. Some want to know this so they can help at home, some want to know what questions to ask, and others want to make sure their children are progressing as expected. Teachers in standards-based classrooms have *lots* of information about learning to share, and we caution you to work with families to determine the level of information that is most useful and desired.

The level of detail we need as teachers is not always what parents need or want and can lead to overload, frustration, and disconnection.

- **Unit and/or Marking Period Reports:** During these formal reporting periods, teachers will have the most accurate summative data about the learning targets to report. It's important to let parents and students know that while summative, these current levels of achievement are only that—current. They can change as the learning changes. Make sure there is a simple key with explanations of what they will see as well as any other contextual information that is relevant to the report. When sending a standards-based report home for the first time, we highly recommend an e-mail or letter prior to receiving it and an opportunity for questions or feedback after receiving it.

- **Portal:** Many SBG tools offer a portal, where parents and students can check their progress and achievement whenever they want. This can be confusing to parents new to SBG, particularly if you previously had a portal based on completion and points. Be sure to clearly communicate to parents and students about what will be updated and when, how it's different than an assignment-based portal, and all of the other ways they have to see how their students are doing in your class.

There is no single tool that can quickly and comprehensively communicate all of the above purposes at the same time, and wishing that the standards-based gradebook tool could take care of it all will only lead to frustration for everyone. Developing new and effective ways to communicate with our families during the transition to a standards-based system may be a bit more time-consuming initially, but making sure that families feel included during the changes will provide the safety and trust we all need to improve learning. See Figure 10.3 for ideas on how to communicate with families.

FIGURE 10.3 Communicating With Families

Example: This example is for a middle school team of four teachers and 80 students who use JumpRope as their standards-based tracking and reporting program.			
Type of Communication	**How will we communicate?**	**When will we communicate?**	**Who will be responsible?**
Personal Connections	• Postcards home; we will keep a checklist of students to ensure that we contact each student's family. • Brief, personal comments on JumpRope	By the end of the first two weeks, we will have sent a postcard to every student's family. After that, we will try to send one per trimester to each student. We will post comments in JumpRope at trimester time.	Each teacher will be responsible for sending 20 postcards throughout the first two weeks; after that, we will choose 5–10 students per week at our weekly team meeting and split up the task of contacting these students' families.

Type of Communication	How will we communicate?	When will we communicate?	Who will be responsible?
Curriculum	• Team website	We will update our website biweekly and send a group e-mail reminder to our parents.	Each trimester, a different teacher will be responsible for ensuring that the website update happens. By the second trimester, student teams will take over updates, overseen by the teacher in charge.
Habits and Behaviors	• E-mail from student to family; this includes an update on what they're learning, highlights of the week, upcoming events or assignments, and a personal reflection. Students will cc the homeroom teacher. • Other contact as necessary for significant behavior or habit concerns.	Students will send e-mails every Friday during homeroom time; the first month will probably require 30 minutes, but after that, it may take less time.	Homeroom teachers will run and organize this for their 20 students, providing guidance as necessary.
Learning	• JumpRope portal • JumpRope reports	The portal will be ongoing, and reports are sent at the end of each trimester.	**Individual teachers:** Enter data biweekly about academic learning targets and ensure that summative data is ready at trimester time. **Team:** Enter summary data about agreed-upon habit targets. **School:** Print/format/send reports to families.

Challenges

Finding a Balance: When communicating with families about changing practices in your classroom or school, we want to be honest without causing undue and unnecessary stress or confusion. Teaching is our profession, so we have a deeper understanding of learning and pedagogy than most of our families will, but their own experience in school can often lead the public to think they have as much experience and expertise as we do. When they hear about changes that seem to fly in the face of their own (often successful) school experiences, parents can quickly get defensive. There were formulas for success that worked for many of our parents that we now know may no longer be relevant, but convincing parents to trust us on this can be akin to asking them to let us take their kid skydiving without a parachute. In order to address these fears, our communication may initially have to highlight what stays the same rather than focusing on what will change. For example, by letting families of juniors and seniors know that their students' transcripts will still look the same to colleges for the next few years—and that they will still include a GPA and letter grades—parents were much more willing to support internal changes in instruction, assessment, and reporting. Transparency is important, but knowing how, when, and how much to communicate may prevent anxiety and allow transformation.

Combatting Old Communication Systems: If your school has just transitioned from a traditional online gradebook to a standards-based gradebook, there may be some pressure from parents to continue to report the types of information they are used to receiving. Many traditional gradebooks are organized by assignment rather than learning target, making it easy to track and report compliance. Parents and students (and teachers) get used to this. These gradebooks let families know what has been turned in and what is missing. They allow parents to check compliance nightly. They allow students to see learning as a collection of points, a game that leads to rewards or punishments at home and at school. Before online portals, parents did not have daily updates about their kids, but in the name of transparency, we trained them to think they need it to stay on top of their student's learning. That's not true, and we can retrain them to focus on the learning, communicating missing work when (and only when) it becomes an issue for that learning. You may have to stand up to some parents early in the year, and that's why having a comprehensive communication plan is so important.

The Guilt-Free Box

Overwhelmed by the idea of communicating in multiple ways? Stressed out by the thought of developing new and possibly technologically complicated systems? Start small.

- Send one personal e-mail home per kid per year—just one, and it can be brief. Make it positive and related to something specific that the student did in your class or that you observed.

- One time during your next unit, either send a group e-mail to parents (if you have a parent e-mail list made) or ask your students to take home a note that describes what students will be doing in your class or what they have just done. Let it be celebratory and brief!

Conclusion

*Imagine the Possibilities, or Romancing
Standards-Based Learning*

We've been thinking a lot lately about why standards-based learning (SBL) is so important. For the past eight years, this has been almost our sole focus, first as classroom teachers trying to make it work and then as instructional leaders, helping others make it work. And after almost a decade, we are not yet burnt out; in fact, despite frustrations and obstacles and curveballs and exhaustion, we are more energized than ever. Why?

> **Because SBL has the potential to transform education in really cool and important ways.**

If you haven't yet watched Dr. Robert Duke's (2008) amazing lecture at Cornell University, clear your schedule for the next hour and do so. It's called "Why Students Don't Learn What We Think We Teach" and, centered within 50 minutes of insight and humor, he talks about the balance between romance and precision. So often, Duke says, we think learners need to master the details—precision—before they can truly experience the romance of a discipline or a subject or a topic. But the problem is that precision is hard. It requires patience and perseverance and reflection. It requires sweat and failure and doubt. All of that is important—vital, actually—but why on earth would anyone struggle through all of that precision? Why take the time to sweat and fail and doubt and practice and reflect and repeat? Because of the romance. Because of the possibilities that precision opens up.

The same is true of SBL. It's so easy to get caught up in the precision of the transformation and forget the romance. We spend so much time on targets and scales and assessments and reporting; we dive into the measuring and the calibrating and the tracking so that we can more accurately communicate about learning. This is all vital. And it's hard. So hard. We want teachers to be patient, to be reflective, to persevere, to fail, to sweat, and to keep trying. We say it's better for learning (true) and that it will improve engagement (true) and that we will have much more honest and clear communication (true). But if we don't balance that precision with the romance of experience and possibility, then we risk getting lost in the details and losing sight of what can be.

Romance comes, in part, from experiencing success. In order to persevere, a struggling musician needs to feel what it's like to make beautiful music, not only hear it made by someone else. With the transition to SBL, teachers need to feel what it's like when it's working in order to keep trying and tweaking and struggling when it's not. So, if you're a teacher, allow yourself to dive deep with one small element of this process in order to reach that level of success rather than trying to get better at everything at once. If you are an administrator, do everything you can to remove obstacles for your teachers so that they can feel successful—give them release time to collaborate, be an extra body in the classroom to help manage, and take on some of the challenging parent and student communication so your teachers don't have to. Most teachers we know are already so hard on themselves, seeing only the problems with the class they taught instead of the many highlights and worrying about the one student they didn't reach rather than celebrating the 24 they did. Feeling success with SBL may be difficult for a while, but without that feeling, it can be tough to keep going. Find someone to celebrate with.

Romance also comes from imagining possibilities, and that's how we want to end our time with you. Set aside those targets, scales, gradebooks, K-U-Ds (know, understand, do), and common assessments for a few minutes and let yourself be romanced. Imagine the possibilities that SBL allows!

Imagine if we had no bells.

What if the schedule were driven by interest and need rather than by bells? Bells were instituted in schools to efficiently move large numbers of students in and out of classrooms. They are a system of control that signify the start and/or end of usually equal blocks of time someone has determined is necessary. Google bell schedules and poke around at the first few links you find. Here are some interesting things we found:

- A school in Connecticut: 5th period is from 12:13–1:06
- A school in California: Period 2 is 8:48–9:36
- A school in Arizona: Period 6 is 11:19–12:12

In some schools, bells ring every 28 minutes (to accommodate middle and high school needs with a single bell system), some ring every 53 minutes, and some ring every 90 minutes. In some schools, there is a bell to signify the start of class, a bell to signify the end of class, and a warning bell to signify that the bell that will signify the start of the *next* class is about to ring. When you stop to think about it, it's nuts. When was the last time you met a friend for lunch at 12:13? When was the last time you had a meeting with your financial planner at 9:36? How can any learner, particularly adolescent learners, be expected to reach any understanding or depth when switching activities every 28 or 42 or 53 or even 87 minutes?

We could overhaul the schedule. Imagine what it could look like (and sound like!) if students moved when we and they determined it was time, based on learning needs and interest. Students might build their own weekly or monthly schedules (with help from an advisor) and may spend 28 minutes on certain tasks and three hours on others.

> SBL could help us do this. If we have a way to track and monitor learning—and if students understand their own strengths and challenges more than they ever have—then we no longer have to live by the bell. If we are working together as a school on transferable skills, then we will no longer need to chunk the day into equal-size blocks; we can instead flex our time to meet the needs of our learners.

What would it look like? How would it be organized? What are the obstacles? No idea. But imagine if we could figure it out.

Imagine if we had no disciplines.

What if we didn't sort learning into content areas? Content or discipline areas allow us to organize sets of knowledge, skills, and understandings into manageable silos. Students talk about having *history work*, doing *English*, or going to *science class*. But we all know that's not real. None of us breaks our days into disciplines. Sure, we focus on different types of tasks throughout the day, but could you actually label your tasks based on discipline? Scientists do science, but aren't they also communicating through writing (English), calculating (math), looking at historical precedence (history), and graphically expressing findings (art)? Writers are writing, but aren't they also pitching their ideas (public speaking), researching background (science or history), and, depending on the topic of the writing, incorporating all sorts of other content areas? Life is not sorted by discipline.

We could reorganize learning. Imagine what it would feel like to be in a building organized by topics or themes rather than disciplines. Students might be based in a sustainability hub, working to solve problems and make the community a better place. To do so, they would need to learn relevant math and history and science and art and language, but these would all now be in service to the central theme or topic. Teachers with expertise in certain areas would do deep dives with students, acting as mentors and facilitators and, even at times, lecturers.

> SBL could help us do this. Hubs would need to be grounded in transferable skills, and together we would work to create learning targets that help students push their current abilities and challenge existing understandings. Students could track their own learning (with lots of guidance and help from the teachers), set goals, and reflect constantly; we could graduate students who are curious, self-directed, and who are not only prepared to change the world but have already been doing so.

What would it look like? How would it be organized? What are the obstacles? No idea. But imagine if we could figure it out.

Imagine if school never closed.

What if our schools were always open? Many New Englanders (often college students with thermoses full of coffee) have made the middle-of-the-night trek to Freeport, Maine, to visit the flagship L.L. Bean store. While they could have made the drive in the morning or afternoon, knowing that they could show up at 2:00 in the morning was novel enough that it made it irresistible. If you aren't from New England, you may not know that the store in Maine doesn't have locks on the doors. They are always open—weekends, nights, holidays, 24 hours a day, 365 days a year.

Most schools open their doors around 7:00 a.m. and close around 4:00 p.m., with exceptions for some club or sporting events. This is true five days a week, 181 days a year. There may be a few summer school classes or an innovative evening class for students, but for the most part, school runs at predictable and regular times for limited hours, days, and weeks. And the rest of the time, the building sits empty.

We could reimagine the days. Imagine what it would be like to come into the building on a Saturday morning and see dozens of students and a handful of teachers working on a project together. Students might decide they need access to the stage, so they sign up and show up. A teacher might decide to run a three-hour workshop on a Tuesday night for anyone who wants to attend—students or community members. The school might decide to offer night classes for juniors and seniors who need their sleep during the day or who want to be part of internships. Families could learn together in the summer, community organizations could take advantage of the facilities, teachers could pursue their own learning, and students could offer to teach courses to students. While many of these activities are allowed at schools now—often with special permission and lots of planning and money to pay someone to show up with a key—they could become the norm.

> SBL could help us do this. If we are focused on transferable skills and have ways to document and track learning, then that learning can truly become the constant, and how and when students learn can be so much more creative and flexible.

What would it look like? How would it be organized? What are the obstacles? No idea. But imagine if we could figure it out.

It's exciting to imagine the possibilities for the future of public education. There are so many cool, innovative ideas out there, and even more that no one has thought of yet. Each year, we learn more and more about the brain and learning, and each year, our world changes faster than we ever imagined it could. Each year, we continue to struggle to make changes to our systems that align with what we currently know while anticipating needs for the future. SBL is a result of this learning and this struggle.

We must dive deep into the precision of SBL, learning how to write effective targets and scales, how to assess transferable skills rather than content knowledge, how to instruct students at all different readiness levels, and how to track, report, and respond to the learning. We must dig in and determine the best way to communicate about learning with students, with parents, with colleges, with careers, and with each other. We need to challenge our own experiences and understandings in order to challenge our students.

And all the while, we need to keep doing the daily work of building relationships with our learners and maintaining enough sanity and energy to do this effectively (and sustainably). That's not easy. The precision required for SBL will take time and sweat and failure and perseverance and reflection, and we may even want to give up. That's why we must celebrate success when it happens, continue to imagine the possibilities, and keep the romance alive.

References

Armstrong, T. (2016). *The power of the adolescent brain: Strategies for teaching middle and high school students*. Alexandria, CA: ASCD.

Bruner, J. (2003). *The process of education*. Cambridge, MA: Harvard University Press.

Chappuis, J., Chappuis, S., & Arter, J. (2012). *Classroom assessment for student learning: Doing it right—using it well*. London, UK: Pearson.

Chappuis, S., Commodore, C. A., & Stiggins, R. J. (2017). *Balanced assessment systems: Leadership, quality, and the role of classroom assessment*. Thousand Oaks, CA: Corwin.

Crum, S. (2017, March 29). Standards based learning and special education. *CVU learns: One school's journey to standards-based learning*. Retrieved May 1, 2018, from http://cvulearnsblog.blogspot.com/2017/03/standards-based-learning-and-special.html

Dueck, M. (2014). *Grading smarter, not harder: Assessment strategies that motivate kids and help them learn*. Alexandria, VA: ASCD.

DuFour, R., & Eaker, R. (1998). *Professional learning communities at work*. Bloomington, IN: Solution Tree.

Duke, R. (2008, April 18). *Why students don't learn what we think we teach*. College of Agriculture and Life Sciences (Cals), Cornell University, Ithaca, NY. Retrieved April 29, 2018, from www.cornell.edu/video/robert-duke-why-students-dont-learn-what-we-think-we-teach

Dweck, C. S. (2016). *Mindset: The new psychology of success*. New York, NY: Ballantine Books.

Fisher, D., & Frey, N. (2014). *Better learning through structured teaching: A framework for the gradual release of responsibility* (2nd ed.). Alexandria, VA: ASCD.

Guskey, T. R. (2015). *On your mark: Challenging the conventions of grading and reporting*. Bloomington, IN: Solution Tree Press.

Heath, C., & Heath, D. (2008). *Made to stick: Why some ideas survive and others die*. New York, NY: Random House.

Heath, C., & Heath, D. (2010). *Switch: How to change things when change is hard*. New York, NY: Broadway Books.

Heflebower, T., Hoegh, J. K., & Warrick, P. (2014). *A school leader's guide to standards-based grading*. Bloomington, IN: Marzano Research.

Hiebert, J. (Ed.). (1986). *Conceptual and procedural knowledge: The case of mathematics*. Mahwah, NJ: Lawrence Erlbaum.

Hughes, J. (Director). (1986). *Ferris Bueller's day off*. United States: Paramount Pictures.

Jensen, E. (2008). *Teaching with the brain in mind*. Alexandria, VA: ASCD.

Jung, L. A., & Guskey, T. R. (2012). *Grading exceptional and struggling learners: IEP, RTI, ELL*. Thousand Oaks, CA: Corwin.

Kaplan, R. D. (2014, March 20). Geopolitics and the New World Order. *Time*. Retrieved April 21, 2018, from http://time.com/31911/geopolitics-and-the-new-world-order/

Knight, J. (2016). *Better conversations: Coaching ourselves and each other to be more credible, caring, and connected.* Thousand Oaks, CA: Corwin.

Larmer, J., Mergendoller, J., & Boss, S. (2015). *Setting the standard for project based learning: A proven approach to rigorous classroom instruction.* Alexandria, VA: ASCD.

Moss, C. M., & Brookhart, S. M. (2012). *Learning targets: Helping students aim for understanding in today's lesson.* Alexandria, VA: ASCD.

Nottingham, J. (2017). *The learning challenge: How to guide your students through the learning pit.* Thousand Oaks, CA: Corwin.

O'Connor, K. (2011). *A repair kit for grading: 15 fixes for broken grades.* London, UK: Pearson.

O'Connor, K. (2018). *How to grade for learning: Linking grades to standards.* Thousand Oaks, CA: Corwin.

Pearson, D., & Gallagher, M. (1983, July). The instruction of reading comprehension. *Contemporary Educational Psychology, 8*(3), 317–344.

Popham, W. J. (2001). *The truth about testing: An educator's call to action.* Alexandria, VA: ASCD.

Popham, W. J. (2008). *Transformative assessment.* Alexandria, VA: ASCD.

Popham, W. J. (2010). *Everything school leaders need to know about assessment.* Thousand, Oaks, CA: Corwin.

Reeves, D. B. (2016). *FAST grading: A guide to implementing best practices.* Bloomington, IN: Solution Tree Press.

Rich, B. (2016). *Red house learning.* Retrieved April 29, 2018, from http://www.redhouse learning.com

Schimmer, T., Hillman, G., & Stalets, M. (2018). *Standards-based learning in action: Moving from theory to practice.* Bloomington, IN: Solution Tree Press.

Sousa, D. A. (2017). *How the brain learns.* Thousand Oaks, CA: Corwin.

Stiggins, R. J. (2017). *The perfect assessment system.* Alexandria, VA: ASCD.

Tomlinson, C. A. (2003). *Differentiation in practice.* Alexandria, VA: ASCD.

Tomlinson, C. A. (2016). *The differentiated classroom: Responding to the needs of all learners.* London, UK: Pearson Education.

Tomlinson, C. A., & McTighe, J. (2006). *Integrating differentiated instruction & understanding by design: Connecting content and kids.* Alexandria, VA: ASCD.

Wiggins, G. P., & McTighe, J. (2008). *Understanding by design.* Alexandria, VA: ASCD.

Willis, J. (2006). *Research-based strategies to ignite student learning: Insights from a neurologist and classroom teacher.* Alexandria, VA: ASCD.

Wormeli, R. (2007). *Differentiation: From planning to practice, grades 6–12.* Portsmouth, NH: Stenhouse.

Wormeli, R. (2018). *Fair isn't always equal: Assessing & grading in the differentiated classroom* (2nd ed.). Portsmouth, NH: Stenhouse.

Zull, J. E. (2002). *The art of changing the brain: Enriching teaching by exploring the biology of learning.* Sterling, VA: Stylus.

Index

Figures are indicated by f after the page number.

CORWIN

A SAGE Publishing Company

CORWIN HAS ONE MISSION: to enhance education through intentional professional learning.

We build long-term relationships with our authors, educators, clients, and associations who partner with us to develop and continuously improve the best evidence-based practices that establish and support lifelong learning.

Solutions you want. Experts you trust. Results you need.

AUTHOR CONSULTING

Author Consulting

On-site professional learning with sustainable results! Let us help you design a professional learning plan to meet the unique needs of your school or district. www.corwin.com/pd

INSTITUTES

Institutes

Corwin Institutes provide collaborative learning experiences that equip your team with tools and action plans ready for immediate implementation. www.corwin.com/institutes

ECOURSES

eCourses

Practical, flexible online professional learning designed to let you go at your own pace. www.corwin.com/ecourses

READ2EARN

Read2Earn

Did you know you can earn graduate credit for reading this book? Find out how: www.corwin.com/read2earn